Hey, Bubba!
A Metaphysical Guide to the Good Ol' Boy

David G. Cannon

Illustrated by
Kate Salley Palmer

PEACHTREE PUBLISHERS
Atlanta, Georgia

My thanks to Bill Koon and Corinne Holt Sawyer of
Clemson University who gave valuable suggestions and
that precious commodity, encouragement.
My thanks to Linda Allen who provided help in
preparing the manuscript and more encouragement.

Published by

PEACHTREE PUBLISHERS, LTD.
494 Armour Circle NE
Atlanta, Georgia 30324

Manufactured in the United States of America

10 9 8 7 6 5 4 3 2 1

Library of Congress Cataloging-in-Publication Data

Cannon, David G., date
    Hey, Bubba! A Metaphysical Guide to the Good Ol' Boy /
by David G. Cannon ; illustrated by Kate Salley Palmer.
      p.   cm.
    ISBN 0-934601-90-9 : $7.95
    1. United States--Social life and customs--1971-   --
Humor. 2. Office politics--United States--Humor. 3. Social
networks--United States--Humor.   I. Title.
    E169.04C30   1990
    306.4'0973--dc20   89-26675
                                     CIP

Cover illustration by Kate Salley Palmer
Design by Candace J. Magee

ISBN 0-934601-90-9

CONTENTS

An Official Definition

To Louisiana Fats, Peetalah, Alan, Joe, Cecil, Shala, Big Wamp, Jimmy, and the mob. To Guts, Lard, and Duke—the California mafia. To Sean and Fozzie. And to other Good Ol' Boys everywhere.

May your tribe increase.

An Official Definition

Good Ol' Boy (gŭd ōl bói), n.
Also known as Gobbie (gäbē); pronounced "Gah-bee;"
pl. Gobbies. Male member of Genus Humorosus Hedonistus,
Species Good Timus.
Generally meets the following criteria: 1) fun-loving lifestyle,
2) humorous outlook, 3) unpretentious personal style, 4) sports
fanatic. Found in all geographical locations and cuts across
other sociocultural classifications.

Natural habitat: Often observed at sporting events, in bass
boats, bars, jeeps, and on golf courses.
Synonym: See Yahoo, shitkicker, goat-roper.
Antonym: redneck.

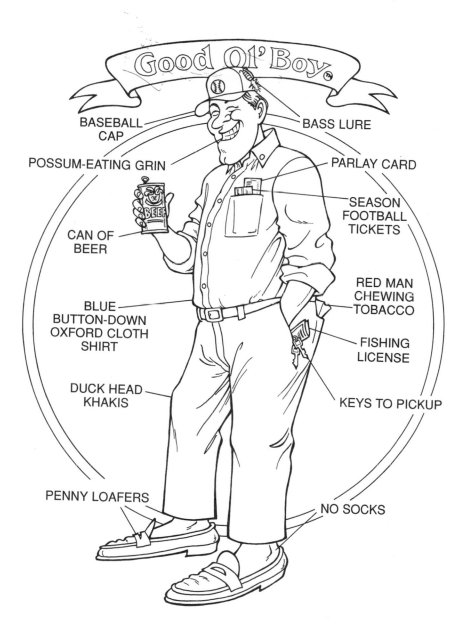

"No need to hurry.
Don't have to scurry.
What, me worry?
I'm a Good Ol' Boy!"

From: *The Rubiyat of Joe Bob Stigall*

CHAPTER ONE

THE RIGHT STUFF

or
In Search of the Good Ol' Boy

THE RIGHT STUFF

In 1989, American manufacturers produced about 160 million baseball caps, and roughly 162 million more were imported.

Yearly sales now approximate one cap for every man, woman, and child in the United States. Radio stations devote more and more time to playing "oldies," and sales of white socks, pickup trucks, and long-neck beer are climbing. Attendance at sporting events is at an all-time high, barbecue restaurants are flourishing, and patriotism is back in style. Pork rinds are *de rigueur* in the Rose Garden, and Cajun food is becoming a national staple. Heroes are back,

STARS AND STRIPES FOREVER

entrepreneurship is again respected, and country and western music enjoys increasing popularity from coast to coast.

At the heart of this cultural and spiritual renaissance is the Good Ol' Boy (a.k.a. Gobbie), a phenomenon as surrounded by mystery and misunderstanding as a possum in a fogbank.

Generally, writers and other media grandees have had about as much success in defining the Gobbie as a hog in ballet class. As a result, stereotypes have rained upon the public consciousness with the dulling plop of hot horse manure hitting asphalt.

The picture presented all too frequently is one of an ignorant Southern lout, a portrayal that misfires on a number of counts. While the Good Ol' Boy has his origins in the South, he is by no means always a Southerner but is in fact found in every corner of the land. Furthermore, he usually isn't stupid, isn't a redneck (see Chapter 4), and doesn't always drive a pickup — though that can certainly be a vehicle of choice. While he definitely doesn't fit the stereotype, defining him can be a task akin to locating hair on a frog.

Basically, the Good Ol' Boy is an anachronism, an old-school cavalier more at home in the age of chivalry than with the "me" generation. He's a traditionalist caught up in a society whose pulse is electronic and whose icons are increasingly plastic. In some corner of his heart, the Gobbie yearns for simpler times when a handshake meant something and getting misty-eyed over the flag was okay. His nostalgia is reflected in his lifestyle, in the straightforward clothes and music he chooses. He disdains the notion that whatever's new and "in" is automatically worth a damn.

While personal loyalty isn't something you'll find the average Good Ol' Boy intellectualizing about over white wine and Brie, he'll typically prove a true and steadfast friend who will circle the wagons with you when things get tough. He forms strong bonds with people and places a high value on old-fashioned camaraderie. His all-weather fidelity to friends makes him a good man to have riding your wing or guarding your flank.

A central part of the Good Ol' Boy's life view is simply that he is no better than anyone else, that while some folks may be more fortunate than others, they're still just folks.

It follows that the Gobbie avoids taking himself (or life) too seriously. He tends to be a plain-spoken, salt-of-the-earth sort who's more concerned with what's in your heart than in your bank account. So sensitive are his antennae to affectation that he will, if highly successful, often talk and dress down in order to avoid appearing biggety (see vocabulary section, Chapter 6).

Not surprisingly, a Good Ol' Boy is more comfortable hob-nobbing with just "plain folks" than with the more glamorous big cheeses. Clint Eastwood, for example, is noted for hanging out with the crew members on his movie sets rather than with the other actor bigwigs. Paul Newman reputedly prefers the comradeship of his racing buddies to the glitzier company of Hollywood poo-bahs.

Generally, a Gobbie has little use for the socially ambitious who try to talk like they're from London when they grew up in Bakersfield. In fact, he often

HIS CUP RUNNETH OVER

views these folks as objects of humor, and his sly wit can prove a deadly pinprick to their affectations.

If social climbing ranks low on his scale of human possibilities, then the opposite is true regarding individualism. A Gobbie typically cuts his own path in life, placing a high premium on his personal freedom. He chafes under the harness of petty rules and regulations so beloved of large organizations. If compelled by necessity to breathe the stale hog's breath of bureaucracy, a Good Ol' Boy will usually find a way to beat the system or at least have some fun with it.

Similarly, he seldom becomes captive to the newest fad or fashion and will spend little time seeking out the latest "in" restaurants or nurturing a fetish for haute mail-order catalogs; mention L.L. Bean to a Gobbie and he'll likely think you're planning to cook up some chili. Mention "avant garde" and he may draw his sword.

Unencumbered by vogue-mongering, our stalwarts choose instead to concentrate on life's more substantial verities like football, fishing, and generally having a good time. In fact, if having a good time were chocolate cake, most Gobbies would be fat. They typically like to have fun and can, alas, at times be undone by their appetites—witness Elvis Presley. By and large, however—though food, drink, and other sublime pursuits loom large on the Good Ol' Boy's personal vista—his is a mellow hedonism, reflecting more a rich enjoyment of life than pedal-to-the-metal abandon. Life's cup is brimming over, and he plans to drink that and order another round.

Saying that a Good Ol' Boy likes sports may rank as the understatement of the decade, much like revealing that bears eat honey and that, yes, they generally crap in the woods. The gaming spirit runs hot in a Gobbie's blood and much of his leisure time is spent either watching, playing, or simply talking about sports. A goodly portion of his social activity will revolve around athletic events, games being great occasions for happy — at times roisterous — gatherings of friends and family. If there's a time when our boy's sports mania peaks, it is football season, and he awaits the arrival of fall with the intensity of a cat at the back door of a fish market.

It comes as no surprise, then, that a primary refuge for the Good Ol' Boy is the outdoors and that he can often be found there hunting, fishing, or otherwise engaged. Strongly drawn to nature, he reflects some of her unfettered qualities in his own personality. It's no accident that he is often described as "down to earth."

The subject of Good Ol' Boys and women is one to be approached with the caution of a racoon tap dancing around a rattlesnake; whatever one says, one's likely gonna get bit by someone. But since any book purporting to define Good Ol' Boys is already perched far out on credibility's shaky limb, why not inch out a bit farther with another bald-faced generalization: women tend to like Good Ol' Boys a lot and for a number of reasons.

First, our lads are basically romantics who tend to fall in love with women (the little black book is not typically a Good Ol' Boy trademark).

Second, they genuinely like women, an appreciation uncluttered by sexual guilt or a lot of pseudo-intellectual blather about how devoted they are to equality. Their honest affinity for females comes across in their good-natured teasing and the small gentilities which acknowledge the differences between the sexes without implying the superiority of either.

Third, Gobbies exude a low-key masculinity for which they don't find it necessary to apologize, openly preferring that women not look and act like men.

Fourth, ours tend to be gallant lads with a touch of old-school chivalry which still appeals to most women.   Good Ol' Boys harken back to a more romantic past when, as the saying goes, "Men were men and women were glad of it."   Perhaps in his secret heart of hearts, every Good Ol' Boy wants to throw his coat down over a mud puddle for a woman to walk on.

It follows that you'll find few closet misogynists among the Good Ol' Boy population.   What you see is what you get. And it won't be half bad.

Well, folks, that's one view of the elephant, this author's perspective on that most elusive phenomenon, the Good Ol' Boy: anachronism, cavalier, sportsman, swashbuckler, rustic, plain fellow, and loyal friend.   And yet still, at least partially, an enigma. Perhaps the mystery at the vibrant heart of the Good Ol' Boy is an essence too gossamer to ever truly capture; perhaps it's no more than an attitude, a generous approach to life that is at once egalitarian, humorous, and self-effacing.

It's been said that Good Ol' Boys never really grow up, that they remain in a state of suspended adolescence.   If that's so, then pass the Clearasil, boys, and read on.   Maybe "adulthood" ain't all it's cracked up to be.

CHAPTER TWO

WE'RE JUST LOOKING FOR A FEW GOOD MEN

or
Yes, Chauncey, You, Too, Can Be a Good Ol' Boy

It's been said the rest of America eventually catches up with the South. This has certainly been the case with regard to politics, country and western music, and cuisine (i.e., Cajun food). In addition, Dixie has at least partially spearheaded the nation's re-enchantment with patriotism and other traditional values typically associated with small-town and rural America. However, the greatest gift from the South to the rest of the country may well be the rise throughout the land of Good Ol' Boyism.

While Southern in origin, the Gobbie phenomenon is now a reality from Savannah to San Diego, from Key West to Brooklyn. Prominent examples of non-Southern Good Ol' Boys include Thomas "Tip" O'Neill and Californians Ronald "Dutch" Reagan, Merle Haggard, and the late John "Duke" Wayne. One can make a strong case that former President John F. Kennedy, for all his Harvard trappings, was really an Eastern Establishment Gobbie and that brothers Bobby and Teddy tried to be, but with far less success. In addition, one suspects that the gracious spirit of the Good Ol' Boy roams free in the heart of William F. Buckley, and that Billy would be a princely companion with whom to pop a few properly chilled pearly tops. Other national examples that come readily to mind are Joe "Willie" Namath, Tom

Selleck, Paul Newman, Clint Eastwood and Sylvester "Sly" Stallone. Joe Willie, a Pennsylvanian, was fortunate enough to have honed his skills under master Good Ol' Boy Paul "Bear" Bryant while at Alabama.

Stallone and Selleck have blended life and art by projecting their private Gobbie personae into popular screen characters. Who can deny that Sly's early film "The Lords of Flatbush" was really a story about a group of Good Ol' Boys from the Bronx? More recently, "Magnum" and "Rocky," with their easy masculinity and laid-back personal styles, have clearly been cut from the Good Ol' Boy mold.

The popular television program "Cheers" centers around a group of northeastern Gobbies hanging out at their favorite watering hole. Sam the bartender, played by actor Ted Danson, is a prototypical Good Ol' Boy. It's no accident that Tip O'Neill did a guest appearance on "Cheers" in which he was shown at the pub drinking beer with the boys!

Looking West, one encounters the cowboy, an "aw shucks" fellow, an unassuming, dirt-kicking, straight-arrow kind of guy who's kind to kids, women, and his horse; in a word, a Good Ol' Boy. One brings to mind Gary Cooper, John Wayne, Alan Ladd, and Johnny Mack Brown (it's doubtful that in real life Ol' Johnny Mack always ordered buttermilk).

Evidence suggests that the phenomenon is alive and well on an international scale. The vastly popular movie "Crocodile Dundee" details the adventures of an Australian Good Ol' Boy transplanted to New York City.

The list of non-Dixie examples could go on and on, but the main point to be made here is that using

14

this handy guide, most men can easily master this dynamic lifestyle. Regardless of where you are from or whether your name is O'Reilly, Fong, Feinstein, or Grabowski; whether you are a Wall Street stock jockey or a jock at 'Bama, a Miami fishmonger or a mover and shaker from Beverly Hills; whether you throw logs in the great Northwest or run hogs in the Midwest; whether you are white, black, red, or brown, *you* can become a Good Ol' Boy!

Preppies, yuppies, and even rednecks have had their respective days in the literary sun. Here at last is a book for Good Ol' Boys, the ultimate connoisseurs of the fine art of being male. The simple steps outlined in this guide will quickly put you on the road to the most exciting lifestyle since the Round Table.

CHAPTER THREE

GOING FOR THE GOLD

or
Using This Manual
to Find Ultimate Fulfillment

The GOOD OL' BOY MOVEMENT WANTS YOU!

Anyone familiar with self-help books can tell you that you have to use them correctly in order to gain the maximum benefit. In short, planned, conscientious effort usually reaps the richest rewards. Here, then, are some serious techniques which should greatly enhance your progress as you work your way through this guide.

1. The Magic of Autosuggestion: As any self-improvement author can attest, one must harness the awesome power of the unconscious mind in order to make it into the winner's circle of life. One way of doing this is through autosuggestion, constantly bombarding your subconscious with positive statements. To utilize this valuable technique, stand each morning gazing at yourself in a mirror. Clutching the *Guide* to your breast, softly chant the following:

"I'm a fun-loving bundle of masculine joy.
A prince among men, I'm a Good Ol' Boy."

(now shaking the hips)

"Hubba-hubba, oogum-boogum,
"Hubba-hubba, oogum-boogum."

Repeat this procedure at least six times each morning for one week. It's advisable to do this in private, lest your squeeze (girlfirend, wife, etc.) or some well-meaning family member have you carted off by the boys with the oversized butterfly net.

2. Mental Imagery: You are more likely to achieve greatness in life if you can first imagine yourself in possession of it. Spend one half hour per day envisioning yourself in various inspirational activities. For example, see yourself reveling with your cronies at a pig roast, catching the Knicks on TV, riding a bar stool at your favorite oasis, or spitting a long, graceful arc of tobacco juice into the sunset. The list of self-improvement activities is limited only by your imagination.

UNLEASHING THE POWER OF THE MIND
(OR: TICKET TO THE FUNNY FARM)

3. Cultural Osmosis: To complement Step 2 and gain first-hand experience, you'll want to start hanging out at beer joints, ball games, golf courses, fishing

21

tournaments, and other spots frequented by Good Ol' Boys. This valuable technique enables you to absorb the flavor of the lifestyle much the same as a roasting possum soaks up barbecue sauce. If married, tell your wife it's all part of your therapy (and make sure you have a good lawyer).

4. The Magic of Goals: Write down goals based on each chapter and read them aloud every night before retiring and each morning when you get up. If this gets boring, intersperse the goals with some "good" passages from a Harold Robbins novel which you have carefully underlined. Even if this exercise doesn't do a lot for your subconscious, it should be great for your libido.

5. Testing Your Knowledge: Take the pop quizzes which are provided at the ends of several chapters. If you score less than 70, have the French maid spank you and take the test again. (You may wish to fail each test several times.) If you don't have a French maid, perhaps your squeeze will fill in.

1) Good Ol' Boyism is like:
   (a)   lumbago.
   (b)   moral bankruptcy.
   (c)   happiness.
   (d)   Keynesian economics.

2) One factor attesting to the rise of Good Ol' Boyism is the increase in sales of:
   (a)   Brie.
   (b)   opera tickets.
   (c)   ballet slippers.
   (d)   pickups and longneck beer.

3) Good Ol' Boys are found:
   (a)   mainly in jail.
   (b)   in the White House.
   (c)   in bread lines.
   (d)   nationwide.
   (e)   both (b) and (d).

4. Good Ol' Boys tend to be:
   (a)   followers of Hari Krishna.
   (b)   at the vanguard of the punk movement.
   (c)   traditional in their outlook.
   (d)   avid collectors of Germaine Greer memorabilia.

5. Good Ol' Boys have been compared to:
   (a)   Fabian socialists.
   (b)   hairdressers.
   (c)   the plague.
   (d)   an old-school cavalier.

6. Mention L.L. Bean to a Gobbie and he'll probably:
   (a)   engage you in a discussion of upscale fashion.
   (b)   think you're hitting him up for a political contribution.
   (c)   think you're talking about a country and western singer.
   (d)   assume you're going to cook up some chili.

7. A Good Ol' Boy is more likely to go to:
   (a)   a Boy George concert.
   (b)   a football game.
   (c)   a marital-enrichment seminar offered by Gary Hart.
   (d)   ballet class.

8. A Gobbie's personality is often described as:
   (a)   the moral equivalent of war.
   (b)   out to lunch.
   (c)   an evil empire.
   (d)   down to earth.

9. Good Ol' Boyism is:
   (a)   a social disease.
   (b)   a life view.
   (c)   evidence of mental breakdown.
   (d)   the end of civilization as we know it.

10. Generally the media have had about as much success in defining the Good Ol' Boy as:
   (a)   an application for food stamps signed by Donald Trump.
   (b)   a hog in ballet slippers.
   (c)   a book entitled Macho Man by Michael Dukakis.
   (d)   a seminar on money management offered by Pete Rose.

Score 10 points for each question answered correctly.
See Appendix for correct answers.

CHAPTER FOUR

SILK PURSES
AND SOW'S EARS

or
Are Good Ol' Boys and
Rednecks Really the Same?

THE GREAT DEBATE

A recent national survey vividly illustrated the importance of the above question in the minds of the American public. Respondents were required to rank in order of importance the six most critical issues facing the country today. The results:

1. The prospect of nuclear war
2. Whether Good Ol' Boys and rednecks are alike
3. The budget deficit
4. Crime
5. Dolly Parton's true bust size
6. Government spending

Many people, including some in the media and others who should know better, use the terms Good Ol' Boy and redneck interchangeably, the implication being that the two are the same. Confusing the two types is an intellectual cow pattie that far too many continue to step in.

It's time to state flat out that Good Ol' Boys aren't rednecks. In fact, the differences between the two are more numerous than fleas on an alley cat.

First, consider the connotations of the terms themselves. The label "redneck" has always implied an ignorant, mean-spirited individual who is constantly looking to start trouble; a charter member of the switchblade and tire-tool set. Ask a knowledgeable person about a redneck joint and he'll invariably tell you that it's dangerous. This picture is the antithesis of the laid-back tolerance of the Good Ol' Boy. Refer to Burt Reynolds or Tom Selleck as Gobbies and most folks will smile in agreement. Describe them as rednecks and you'll likely be regarded as a candidate for the quack shack (also known as the funny farm).

Second, rednecks are almost always found at the bottom of the socioeconomic heap, while Good Ol' Boys inhabit every rung on the ladder from the country club to the executive boardroom (and the Oval Office).

Finally, the Gobbie phenomenon cuts across virtually all groups, while the idea of ethnic rednecks makes as much sense as ballet slippers on a boar hog.

An excellent comparison chart which highlights many of the differences between Good Ol' Boys and rednecks has been provided by MIT professor J. B.

"Greenbeans" Detweiler in his scholarly work *Mythical Implications of Good Ol' Boyism or Don't Hog the Cornbread, Podnuh*. Hopefully, Professor Detweiler's summary will help in permanently laying this issue to rest.

DETWEILER COMPARISON CHART

FACTOR	GOOD OL' BOY	REDNECK
IQ	usually average or above	undetectable
interpersonal style	easy going	pestilential
personality	laid back, fun loving	reptilian
cuisine	loves good food	mistakes Alpo for meat loaf
dress	traditional	"early dirty"
women	genuinely likes them	secretly fears them
social skills	usually advanced	pre-Neanderthal
personal style	humorous, understated masculinity	macho caricature
tradition	cherishes it	no concept of tradition beyond last week's chicken fight
nature	respects and identifies with	uses as a garbage dump

In a word, cabbages aren't kings, apples aren't oranges, and oil and water don't mix. The earth isn't flat, Jane Fonda isn't president of the Conservative Caucus, and, no, Virginia, Good Ol' Boys and rednecks really aren't the same. Take it to the bank.

29

1. Which of the following authors would be likely to recognize the difference between Good Ol' Boys and rednecks?
    (a) Gloria Steinem
    (b) John Kenneth Galbraith
    (c) J. B. "Greenbeans" Detweiler
    (d) Mao Tse-Tung

2. Which of the following men is not referred to as a Good Ol' Boy?
    (a) Tom Selleck
    (b) Sly Stallone
    (c) Truman Capote
    (d) Burt Reynolds

3. Rednecks are described as:
    (a) reptilian.
    (b) pestilential.
    (c) having no detectable IQ.
    (d) all of the above.

4. The redneck lifestyle can be described as:
    (a) upscale.
    (b) downscale.
    (c) scaly.
    (d) both b and c.

5. "Mythical Implications of Good Ol' Boyism or Don't Hog the Cornbread, Podnuh" was written by:
    (a) Kate Millett.
    (b) E. L. Doctorow.
    (c) Leo Tolstoy.
    (d) J. B. "Greenbeans" Detweiler.

6. Redneck hobbies would be likely to include:
    (a) golf.
    (b) chess.
    (c) burglary.
    (d) jogging.

7. Redneck encounter groups are usually held:
    (a) at a therapist's office.
    (b) at the local mental health center.
    (c) at a cloistered retreat.
    (d) in parking lots.

8. Rednecks are more likely to vacation in:
    (a) Puerto Vallarta.
    (b) St. Tropez.
    (c) Monaco.
    (d) the county jail.

9. The Good Ol' Boy's personal style can be described as:
    (a) easy going.
    (b) fun loving.
    (c) unpretentious.
    (d) all of the above.

10. A redneck is more likely to practice his strokes with:
    (a) a tennis racket.
    (b) a putter.
    (c) a tire tool.
    (d) a squash raquet.

CHAPTER FIVE

HEY BUBBA!

or
What's in a Name?

THE PEOPLE'S CHOICE

In your quest for Good Ol' Boy authenticity, it is utterly essential that you have the right kind of name. It must in some way express the eternal adolescence of the Good Ol' Boy as well as his quality of root hog unpretentiousness. Thus you must use the casual form of your name wherever possible and specifically the "y" form of that. For example: Jimmy, not James, Bobby instead of Robert, Solly rather than Sol, Danny for Daniel, Billy for William, Freddy for Frederick, and so on.

A functional middle name is a godsend and should always be used as in Billy Joe, Bobby Lee, Jimmy Lee, Jimmy Ray, Joe Bob, and Johnny Mac.

By all means, acquire a nickname if you don't already have one. Animal names are excellent sources and, if possible, should reflect some aspect of your personality or appearance. Possibilities include Hog, Possum, Crawfish, Chigger, Bear, Frog, Catfish, and Snake. Other popular choices are Bubba, Junior, Red, Little Boy, Cathead, Skeet, Gator Tail, T-Boy, Stump, Peewee, Pear Baby, Chunk, Fat Eye, Slim, Stretch, Speedy, and Gonzo. The list is limited only by your imagination, but be sure your choice is colorful and down to earth.

Pairs of initials used as a first name are particularly appropriate. For example you could be known as J.R., J.T., B.J., R.T., L.Q., or L.C. Initials can be particularly effective when used in conjunction with a nickname, as in L.G. "Moose" Hightower.

If you are a big cheese, and your name's going to appear in the paper, make sure your nickname is included in the middle in quotation marks. For example, you might read Jake "Sonny" Grimesly, Higby "Catfish" Culpepper, or R.T. "Junior" Busby. This is extremely important if you happen to be running for political office. It alerts other Good Ol' Boys to vote for you without having to be diverted by peripheral considerations such as the issues.

34

If your name is something like Philbert, Chauncey, or Fauntleroy, "You in a *heap* of trouble, boy," and prompt remedial action is required. You must quickly take on a nickname or resort to initials or both. An example of such corrective action might be as follows:

Original Name	*Corrected Version*
Chauncey Threldkill McNaughton, III	C.T. "Catfish" McNaughton, III

A number of real-life cases where remedial action was successfully carried out are provided below. Note the immediate improvement in style and panache wrought by the corrected versions.

Original Name	*Corrected Version*
Ronald W. Reagan	Ronnie "Dutch" Reagan
Warren Burger	W. "Bubba" Burger
Richard M. Nixon	Dickie "Beavercheeks" Nixon
Henry Kissinger	H.K. "Catfish" Kissinger
S.I. Hayakawa	S.I. "Peewee" Hayakawa
William F. Buckley	Billy "Sweetpea" Buckley
Luciano Pavarotti	L.Q. "Pork Chop" Pavarotti
Johann Sebastian Bach	Johnny "Baconbutt" Bach
Walter Cronkite	Wally "Gator Tail" Cronkite
William Perry	William "Refrigerator" Perry
George Herbert Walker Bush	George "Owlhead" Bush

Name adjustment is an important step up the ladder to Good Ol' Boy fulfillment. Once your moniker is properly attached, you are ready to move on to the important terrain of proper speech.

CHAPTER SIX

SILVER-TONGUED DEVILS

or
How to Talk

In keeping with our themes of unpretentiousness and self-parody, it's extremely important never to appear uppity in the way you talk. This is extremely true if you happen to be highly educated.

You should therefore avoid using totally correct English. The paradox can be fascinating if you happen to be bright and well educated and talk like you just drove in a herd of goats. This author recalls, for example, his deep admiration at hearing a physician friend shout to a departing patient, "It ain't gonna do you no good if you don't take it reg'lar." So take care to sprinkle your conversation with occasional "ain'ts" and double negatives.

Whatever, you must keep away from the "Three Deadly P's," pretentiousness, preciousness, and pomposity. If you've got anything upstairs, you don't need to sling four dollar words around to try and prove it. Slip into that pseudo-intellectual techno-speak so popular today and you'll end up sounding like a refugee from a middle managers' meeting at IBM. And as for trying to sound cute, regard it as the equivalent of verbal leprosy.

To add color to your speech it's important that you develop your vocabulary. Cogent and up-to-date terms and phrases can add great variety and precision to your speaking style. The following list provides a sampling of appropriate terminology carefully developed within the Good Ol' Boy movement. As you gain a feel for the overall style, you'll be able to carry out further development on your own.

Word or Phrase	Definition and Example of Usage
root hog or die	Difficult: *"Mr. President, getting this bill through Congress is going to be root hog or die."*
to give (someone) a holler	To contact, get in touch with: *"When your lab results come in, Mrs. Carruthers, we'll give you a holler."*
Whatchoo talkin' 'bout?!	An expression of doubt or disagreement: *President to Secretary of State: "A summit this fall? Whatchoo talkin' 'bout, boy?!"*
frogmorton	To kill, croak or really screw over: *"Joe Bob's 'ex' really frogmortoned him in the divorce settlement."*
Gobbie	Good Ol' Boy: *"The President, a confirmed Gobbie, stated that 'This trade imbalance is going to frogmorton our economy.'"*
thowed	Threw: *"The increase in interest rates thowed the market into a tailspin."*
oodlings	A large amount or number of: *"There's oodlings of money to be made in this deal."*
bunch	A whole lot: *"Fannie had a bunch of politicians' names in her appointment book."* Syn: oodlings.
biggety	Snobbish, having an air of superiority: *"She got to acting biggety after coming into her inheritance."*
mess	Sufficient for a meal: *"The senator claimed that he had only gone to Fannie's apartment to cook up a mess of catfish."*
cook up	To prepare, cook: See previous example.
to have something stick in one's craw	To be upset by or disagree with something: *"That particular area of quantum theory sticks in my craw."*
hornswoggle	To dupe, deceive: *"She tried to hornswoggle him into signing over the house."*
grub	Food, cuisine: *"The Chez Paris serves excellent continental grub."*
thote	Throat: *"Upon receiving the news, Jimmy Joe went for his stockbroker's thote."*
goff	Golf: *"Let's play goff tomorrow."*
to put in the wind	To get rid of, dismiss: *"After she met that flamenco dancer, she put her husband in the wind."*

stride	Crotch: *"I tore the stride out of my pants."*
wimmin	Females: *"Some good-looking wimmin hang out there."*
pearly top	A cold beer: *"Following the initial round of talks, the President and General Secretary Gorbachev reportedly retired to the Rose Garden to pop a few pearly tops and eat pork rinds."*
ground squirrel	Chipmunk: *"I wonder if those ground squirrels are good to eat."*
to blow the gaff	To inform on, give information, squeal, sing: *"She went to the IRS and blew the gaff on Bobby Lee."*
to crawfish	To hedge, waffle, equivocate: *"It appears the House has begun to crawfish on the budget compromise."*
birddog	V., to chase women: *"She claimed she shot him because of his birddogging."*
plum give out	Extremely fatigued, exhausted: *"Observers at the summit described the Chairman as appearing plum give out."*
squeeze	N., Female with whom one is romantically involved; i.e., wife or girlfriend: *"The president and his squeeze attended the diplomatic reception."*
sho' nuff	Extremely, very, really: *"This legislation will be sho' nuff efficacious in promoting capital formation in the basic industries sector."*
Moody's goose	N., The fastest creature alive: *"Upon receipt of a genuine proposal, this government is prepared to approach the bargaining table with the speed of Moody's Goose."*
whip out	N., Money, ready cash: *"In testimony before the Senate Finance Comittee, the Treasury Secretary stated that without substantial spending cuts, the government would experience a serious shortfall in whip out in the current fiscal year."*
tall hog at the trough	The boss, head man, big cheese: *"The President stated that with regard to the direction and implementation of foreign policy, the Secretary of State would be tall hog at the trough."*

The use of certain abbreviations can add precision and efficiency to your speech. The suggestions
below form a core to which you can add as you
become more proficient.

Abbreviation	Definition	Example
D.T.E	Down to earth	"Just keep it D.T.E."
C.B.S.	Cut the bullshit	"Come on, counselor, just C.B.S."
F.O.G.	Feet on the ground	"In fiscal policy, we have to keep our F.O.G."
G.G.L.	Gobbie good life	"We must remain ever vigilant in our defense of liberty and the G.G.L."
T.C.B.	Taking care of business	"When you called, we were T.C.B."
B.L.	Bottom line	"Just get to the B.L."

Frequent use of the following words and terms
can serve to identify you as a pretentious twit and are
best avoided:
interface
input
prioritize
social agenda
social justice (avoid unless you are a politician and
   then use this term only in support of personal gain
   or pet porkbarrel projects)
social relevance
the public interest (use only if you work for a
   governmental bureaucracy and then only to camouflage grievous bungling or folly)
moonbeam (as a name)
parameter
time frame
artistic fulfillment (may be used only if you're an
   out-of-work TV actor appearing on the Carson
   show)

42

1. A Good Ol' Boy's name should reflect:
   (a) his level of social awareness.
   (b) his commitment to the arts.
   (c) his shoe size.
   (d) his quality of root hog unpretentiousness.

2. Which of the following is most likely a Good Ol' Boy?
   (a) Philbert Winstead
   (b) Chauncey Dortmunder
   (c) Harvey Quintillian, III
   (d) R.J. "Catfish" Culpepper

3. A colorful nickname is:
   (a) evidence of mental incompetency.
   (b) a badge of Good Ol' Boy authenticity.
   (c) grounds for divorce.
   (d) evidence of membership in a subversive organization.

4. If you are running for political office, a good nickname can:
   (a) lead to impeachment.
   (b) insure the Polish vote.
   (c) alert other Good Ol' Boys to vote for you.
   (d) prompt your wife to vote for your opponent.

5. Your speaking style should convey the impression that:
   (a) you teach a course in Rhetoric 101.
   (b) you just drove in a herd of goats.
   (c) you've memorized Roget's *Thesaurus*.
   (d) you're addressing a formal tea for the executive committee of NOW.

6. Slip into pseudo-intellectual technospeak and you'll sound like:
   (a) a pompous twit
   (b) a middle manager at IBM.
   (c) a government bureaucrat.
   (d) all of the above.

7. In speaking, one must always avoid the appearance of being:
   (a) literate.
   (b) from New Jersey.
   (c) knowledgeable about anything.
   (d) uppity.

8. Chronic cuteness is the equivalent of:
   (a) verbal leprosy.
   (b) appearing on a nationally televised lip-sync contest with your fly open.
   (c) having breath like a dead hog.
   (d) going to accept the Heisman Trophy in drag.

9. Which of the following terms describes services regularly provided to the people by Congress?
   (a) hornswoggling
   (b) frogmortoning
   (c) crawfishing
   (d) all of the above

10. Developing your Good Ol' Boy vocabulary will:
   (a) lead to incarceration.
   (b) guarantee you an appearance on the Phil Donahue show.
   (c) add color to your speech.
   (d) lead to your arrest as an illegal alien.

Score 10 points for each question answered correctly.
See Appendix for correct answers.

CHAPTER SEVEN

"Why should I adorn myself like a popinjay? I wear my accoutrements on my soul."

—*Cyrano DeBergerac*

or

How To Dress For Gobbie Success

Reflecting the Gobbie's freewheeling spirit, there is not an inflexible set of rules for you to follow regarding dress. The important thing is to aim for a general tone that is basic and unpretentious. The following Good Ol' Boy styles are presented as general guidelines and points of departure. Thus you have the advantage of several presentations from which you to choose, depending on the situation.

**The
Country
Classic**

This is your standard jeans (Levis preferred), leather belt, and a Big Mac work shirt. With this you'll want a pair of hiking boots, preferably Survivors, but a pair of Sears Roebuck or K mart brogans (for the uninitiated, *Webster's* describes a brogan as a "coarse leather work shoe reaching to the ankle") will do nicely. The look is rugged and outdoorsey. In winter you can switch to a flannel shirt and a leather, plaid, or corduroy jacket. Top things off with a John Deere, Caterpillar, or Budweiser cap and you're in business. The *piece de resistance* is to plug a chaw of Redman in your mouth. The important "Double Cup" technique of chewing tobacco and drinking beer at the same time is covered in a later section. The overall statement here is that "I work for a living, podnuh," but this ensemble is effective even if you don't work—i.e., you are a politician or a commodities broker. For casual social occasions, you can substitute bib overalls for the jeans. A red polka-dot bandanna around your neck is optional. The crowning touch is your favorite baseball cap.

The Cowboy

This getup is ideal for riding a barstool at your favorite beer joint and is time-honored among Good Ol' Boys. The ensemble features cowboy boots (everyone ought to own a pair), jeans, and a western shirt. On the top half, you can substitute a T-shirt or football jersey. Unless you live in a state like Texas, you'll probably want to forget the cowboy hat.

Too ostentatious.

**The
Main Street
Bobby Lee**

You wear a lightweight blue or tan suit (seersucker is okay) with a white or blue button-down Oxford cloth shirt opened at the collar. In cool weather, you can add a V-necked sweater to this. A duck emblem on the sweater is a nice touch that will subtly underline your kinship with the great outdoors. Naturally, you'll want to complete this ensemble with a pair of penny loafers.

For somewhat more casual affairs such as a possum roast, deck shoes that you've hand-rubbed with mink oil are appropriate (Timberlands are nice). You can throw your coat over your shoulder for a slightly more laid-back effect.
This ensemble will serve you well in a variety of settings from the poolroom to your bookie's office.

The Jock

This all-purpose regalia consists of either jeans, sweatpants, or shorts, a sweatshirt or T-shirt, running shoes, and white socks. Top it all off with a baseball cap and you'll be in the swim of things fashion-wise for any kind of athletic undertaking, whether it's doing 12-ounce curls with a cold brew or arm rasslin' the barmaid at your favorite oasis.

49

**The
Jock**

**The
Casual
Clyde**

Great on campus, but suitable for all age groups. You'll go with Duckhead khakis, and a blue or pin-striped Oxford cloth shirt with button-down collar and the sleeves rolled up. Your underpinnings are penny loafers, preferably without socks. Be sure and kick your feet up somewhere, so it'll be obvious that you are sockless (wimmin love this look). Add a blazer to this outfit and you achieve that touch of sartorial paradox which approaches Gobbie nirvana.

The Broadway Jimmy Joe

This regalia is for puttin' on the dog. You start with your basic tuxedo and dress slippers; a white coat and ruffled shirt are optional. The idea here is that your rather humorous ostentation is in itself a self-effacing statement. This look should be accompanied by liberal doses of the possum-eating grin (this important technique is covered in Chapter 10), which informs others that you aren't taking all this too seriously. Still, you can enjoy your splendor and the reactions of others to the paradox between your glad rags and your down-to-earth style. Take care to use incorrect English when wearing this outfit and consider chewing tobacco and wearing a baseball cap as nice optional touches.

A variation on this theme is a three-piece suit, a Fedora with a feather, and a black umbrella, unopened, of course. Utilize this for the homecoming game or the local horsey set's "Cup Classic," where the real purpose is eating, drinking, and looking at each other's clothes.

In addition to knowing what to wear, it is important to have a feel for attire that is regarded as somewhat less than optimal. The following definitely fall into that category and should be regarded as the sartorial equivalent of hives.

Transvestism
The "lounge lizard" look
    (see below)
Most anything made of
    100-percent polyester
Earrings
Platform shoes

Punk
Handbags
Orange hair
T-shirt with logo
    "Sex Instructor—
    First Lesson Free"
Nose pins
Mohawk haircut

The Lounge Lizard

Also taboo is a popular style known in fashion circles as the "Lounge Lizard." This consists of paisley shirt open nearly to the waist, gold chains around the neck, an earring in one ear, thin white belt, tight polyester pants, and either suede, patent leather, or white slip-on shoes.

The guidelines presented in this chapter should quickly transform you into a tall hog at the trough among the fashion-minded elite. It's now time to turn your attention to that ultimate repository of culinary delight, Good Ol' Boy cuisine.

52

"...the rosy glow of eventide on the flower-covered wall of a rustic restaurant, the feeling of hunger, the yearning for women, the pleasant sensation of luxury..."

—Marcel Proust,
REMEMBRANCE OF THINGS PAST

or

What To Eat

THE DANGER ZONE

Contrary to macho myth, Good Ol' Boys typically like to cook and are usually adept at it. As in other areas, the emphasis is on basic fare, although Gobbies will eat about anything that doesn't eat them and even a few critters that do. The bottom line is that a Good Ol' Boy eats something because he enjoys it, not because it's trendy or he'll look good eating it. As with other things, his approach is utilitarian: if it tastes good, eat it. Good food is good food, whether it's fancy French grub or the famous Mayonnaise Fold-over.

Now that the general guidelines have been provided, here are some down-home favorites that are extremely quick and simple to prepare. These classics will be followed by a few more elaborate recipes in case you're throwing a state dinner or a diplomatic reception at your local beer joint. These concoctions will give you an overall flavor of Good Ol' Boy cuisine, putting you well on the road to culinary self-actualization.

Quick Favorites

CORNBREAD PARISIENNE
Fill a tall glass halfway up with crumbled-up cornbread prepared from a standard packaged mix. Now fill the glass the rest of the way up with buttermilk. Eat with a spoon. Hog heaven is only a bite away.

CORNBREAD MEXICANA
Do the same as above but this time make the cornbread with "Martha White's Mexican Cornbread Mix." This has jalapeno peppers and other good stuff in it and will give you a near peak experience. For extra excitement, add 1/2 teaspoon Tabasco sauce to the batter. Olé, boy!

BANANA SANDWICH
Slice a ripe banana into quarter-inch slices, cutting horizontally, not vertically. Liberally spread two pieces of bread with mayonnaise. Heap the banana slices on one piece and cover it with the other.

BANANA SANDWICH ST. TROPEZ
This is a deluxe variation on the standard version. Slice the banana as above but put mayo on only one piece of bread. Spread the other piece with crunchy peanut butter. Place the banana slices on the bread with the peanut butter and then sprinkle raisins on top of that. Cover with other piece of bread and you're on the threshold of culinary ecstasy.

56

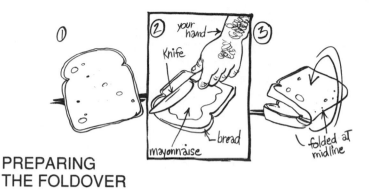

PREPARING
THE FOLDOVER

MAYONNAISE FOLD-OVER À LA HITCHCOCK

This tour de force is from the kitchens of master chef Cecil Hitchcock. Take a piece of white sandwich bread, the kind that's supposedly not good for you. Spread it liberally with mayonnaise and fold it over at the midline. Eat.

CHEESE GRITS

Cook some grits as per instructions on the package. While they are simmering, grate a healthy portion of sharp cheddar cheese into the bottom of a bowl. Pour the piping hot grits over the cheese and allow the whole mess to sit for two minutes. Stir and eat.

GREEN BEANS CHAMPS ELYSÉES

Break up a mess of string beans and bring to a boil in enough water to cover them. Reduce heat and add either several strips of bacon, a slab of salt pork, or several ham hocks. Simmer until beans are very tender, usually about 2 hours. Canned green beans can be used in emergencies. Add water as necessary.

LIMA BEANS FLORENTINE

Simmer fresh limas with ham hocks about 3 hours. The lima beans create their own succulent gravy which you then pour with the beans over hot cornbread, or Cornbread Mexicana if you're feeling sporty. Excellent with a glass of cold buttermilk.

Standard Recipes

There is little doubt that the cuisine you serve will in large measure determine the social impact of your soirees ("Another serving of Hog Jowl Surprise, Mrs. Dupont?"). This section featuring "blue chip" fixings is provided as a reference for those special occasions when you have to lay out a more elaborate trough, and should keep you in the vanguard of the gastronomic elite.

HOG JOWL SURPRISE

2 1-lb. cans blackeyed peas
1 large red onion, chopped
3 cloves garlic, chopped
1 lb. smoked hog jowl
1 teaspoon salt
1 teaspoon black pepper
1 teaspoon Tabasco sauce, or to taste
1 cup rice
2 bay leaves
1/2 teaspoon parsley
1/2 teaspoon thyme
2 green peppers, chopped
1/3 cup safflower oil
2 cups pork-flavored bouillion (you can get by with water)

Sauté the onion, garlic, and green peppers in the oil until tender. Cut the hog jowl into chunks and dump it in, browning it for a couple of minutes. Pour all this into a large pot. Cook the rice and add it to the pot. Throw in the blackeyed peas, all the spices, and the bouillion. Simmer on low heat for 30-45 minutes, stirring frequently. Add more water (or bouillion) as needed. This dish is traditionally eaten on New Year's Day to bring good luck in the coming year. One bite of this delicacy and you'll know that your good fortune has already begun.

REDEYE CHILI

2 lbs. lean ground beef
1 lb. pork sausage, "hot" blend
3 1-lb. cans stewed tomatoes
1 16-oz. can tomato sauce
2 green peppers, chopped
1 large red onion, chopped
3 cloves garlic, chopped
2 1-lb. cans kidney beans, drained
1/2 teaspoon EACH cumin, thyme, oregano,
        black pepper, basil leaves
1 tablespoon dill seed, crushed
1 teaspoon Tabasco sauce (or more to taste)
1 tablespoon dill weed, crushed
3 bay leaves
1 1/2 tablespoons chili powder
1/2 cup safflower oil

Brown the ground beef and sausage, pouring off the fat.
Sauté the onion, garlic, and green pepper in the safflower
oil until tender. Pour them, with the oil and the meat, into
a large pot. Add the stewed tomatoes, tomato sauce, and
all the spices. Simmer this mess for 2-3 hours, stirring
frequently. Of course, part of the fun of cooking chili is
tasting and improvising as you go along. You can add
more Tabasco sauce or use interesting meat variations
such as ground buffalo, bear, venison, or possum. Serve
this with cornbread and buttermilk and blast off into
culinary orbit.

PIMENTO BURGER RODEO DRIVE

For more formal occasions, the trusty pimento burger is
a long-time favorite of Gobbie gourmands. Start off with
lean ground beef, about 1/3 lb. for every hamburger you'll
be making. Add 2 tablespoons of teriyaki or soy sauce per
pound of meat and mix well. Shape into patties and
charbroil or fry until the inside is a nice pink. Steam some
large onion rolls or sesame seed buns, using a saucepan

and steaming rack. Generously lard each side of the bun with mayonnaise and place a patty on each bun. Now heap a liberal coating of pimento cheese on each patty. Add lettuce, tomato, salt, and pepper to taste and you're in business.

Dr. Dave's Fried Chicken and Gravy

Chicken

1 3-lb. frying chicken, cut up
1 tablespoon sugar
1 cup buttermilk
1 1/2 cups safflower oil
1 cup flour
Medium-size brown paper bag
2 teaspoons salt
1 teaspoon black pepper
1 egg (optional)

In the paper bag, mix together the flour, salt, pepper, and sugar. Mix the buttermilk and egg together in a shallow dish. Dip the chicken pieces into the buttermilk mixture and then place them in the bag, two or three at a time. With the top of the bag folded over and firmly held, shake until the chicken is well coated. Fry the chicken in the oil very slowly in a heavy, covered skillet. Turn as necessary, but otherwise keep covered, with the heat just high enough to maintain slow frying. When the meat separates easily from the bone with a fork, remove from heat and place on a covered platter to keep warm. With the same skillet, proceed as below to prepare the gravy.

Gravy

2-3 tablespoons oil from the frying
3 tablespoons flour
1 teaspoon salt
1/2 teaspoon black pepper
2 cups milk (nonfat is O.K.)

Over medium heat, brown the flour in the oil, adding the salt and pepper. As the flour browns, add the milk, and stir until gravy begins to thicken. Remove from heat and serve.

FAT HARRY'S CHICKEN BOG

1 3-lb. stewing chicken
3 stalks celery, cut up
2 cups rice, uncooked
1 large red onion, chopped
3 cloves garlic, chopped
1 lb. mushrooms, sliced
2 large green peppers, chopped
1 lb. smoked sausage, sliced
2 chicken bouillion cubes
1/4 cup safflower oil
salt, pepper, and cayenne to taste

Barely cover the chicken with water in a large pot (a crockpot is ideal). Add the chopped celery and bouillion cubes. Cover and slowly stew until the bird is extremely tender. Debone the chicken and chop into small pieces, reserving the cooking broth and celery. Cook the rice. In a large pot, slightly brown the sausage, pouring off the fat. Add the onion, garlic, green pepper, mushrooms, and oil and sauté until tender. To this add the chicken, rice, celery, spices, and 1 cup of broth. Heat for 10 minutes on low, stirring frequently. Additional amounts of broth may be added as needed.

BARBEQUED RIBS

1 bottle mesquite-flavored barbeque sauce (your choice)
Tabasco sauce
Farmer style pork ribs

Simmer the ribs in water over low heat until very tender. Place ribs in a shallow dish. Unless the barbeque sauce is already labeled "hot," add Tabasco sauce to taste (preferably 'til the hairs stand up on the back of your neck). Liberally coat the ribs with the sauce and cook over charcoal, basting with additional sauce until nicely browned.

62

Louisiana Fats' Baked Beans

3 1-lb. cans pork and beans
1/2 cup barbecue sauce
1/3 cup black molasses
2 tablespoons honey
1 teaspoon Tabasco sauce
1 large red onion, chopped
1 lb. bacon
1/4 cup safflower oil

Fry the bacon, drain, and break up into pieces. Sauté the onion in the safflower oil until tender and lightly browned. Now dump everything into a lightly oiled baking dish, mix, and bake at 325 degrees for 20-30 minutes. Optionally, you can simmer this mess on very low heat on top of the stove, taking care to stir frequently.

A Possum and a Six-Pack

An all-time favorite from the kitchens of noted gourmand Bill Koon. Roast one possum until tender. Eat possum and drink six-pack. Additional six-packs may be added to taste.

Well, that's it for grub. These helpful hints should launch you on the road to five-star culinary renown.

Pop Quiz 4

1. Good Ol' Boys are often accused of being in a state of:
   (a) inebriation.
   (b) catatonia.
   (c) moral disarray.
   (d) suspended adolescence.

2. The rise of Good Ol' Boyism has been likened to:
   (a) a plague.
   (b) a renaissance.
   (c) the end of civilization as we know it.
   (d) entropy.[1]

3. When the going gets rough, a Good Ol' Boy is likely to:
   (a) call out the National Guard.
   (b) call out Zsa Zsa Gabor.
   (c) circle the wagons with you.
   (d) bow toward Mecca.

4. Good Ol' Boys are more likely to buy:
   (a) season football tickets.
   (b) a book on humanitarianism by Leona Helmsley.
   (c) an inspirational video tape featuring Jim and Tammy Faye Bakker.
   (d) an album of Gregorian chants by Nancy Reagan.

5. An indicator of the Good Ol' Boy movement has been a rise in:
   (a) the divorce rate.
   (b) flatulence.
   (c) the sale of longneck beer.
   (d) the number of Henny Youngman fan clubs.

6. Good Ol' Boys would more likely be found attending:
   (a) a seminar on Ethics in Government by Jim Wright.
   (b) a golf tournament.
   (c) a conference on Third World poetry.
   (d) a lecture on postmodernism in feminist art.

7. Defining the Good Ol' Boy can be as difficult as:
   (a) locating hair on a frog.
   (b) locating an honest politician.
   (c) figuring out the government's fiscal policy.
   (d) all of the above.

8. Good Ol' Boys are more likely to read:
   (a) a political primer co-authored by Jane Fonda and Vanessa Redgrave with foreword by Manuel Noriega.
   (b) the memoirs of Idi Amin.
   (c) *Sports Illustrated*
   (d) a book on etiquette by Mike Tyson.

9. Good Ol' Boy cuisine is likely to:
   (a) be utilitarian.
   (b) require an environmental impact statement.
   (c) register 4 on the Richter Scale.
   (d) produce acid rain.

10. Cornbread Mexicana refers to:
   (a) a famous Mexican basketball player.
   (b) a Good Ol' Boy recipe.
   (c) a renowned Latino actress.
   (d) the Mexican national dance.

[1]The degredation of the matter and energy in the universe to an ultimate state of inert uniformity.

Score 10 points for each question answered correctly.
See Appendix for correct answers.

CHAPTER NINE

"I'm like a Mississippi bullfrog
Sittin' on a hollow stump.
I got so many women
I don't know which-a-way to jump."

—Big Joe Turner,
"FLIP, FLOP AND FLY"

or

Choosing a Mate (Or Mates)

DECISIONS, DECISIONS

Picking suitable feminine companionship can be one of the most challenging tasks facing the Good Ol' Boy. Finding someone (or several someones) with the looks of Cheryl Tiegs, the patience of Job, and the sexual skills of Mata Hari, not to mention the football savvy of Phyllis George, can be daunting even to the most skilled birddogger.

There are a number of qualities you'll be seeking in addition to the above. You'll want a gal who's down to earth, has a good sense of humor, and likes sports and good food. Beware of social climbers and tight-lipped types from the lunatic wing of the feminist movement. Also avoid fashion-mongers unless they buy their own clothes. Ideally, your choice will consider penny loafers and jeans to be "haute couture." Look for casual, laid-back sexiness, a girl who can be one of the boys and yet remain unabashedly feminine.

Before entering into any significant relationship with a woman, by all means fill out the following rating scale. Most women will applaud your rational approach and gladly consent to the necessary interview.

THE COMPANION SUITABILITY SCALE—Part A

Place a check beside each item which seems to fit the woman being evaluated. Score 1 point for each item checked and record the total score at the bottom. The endorsement of a single item in this section is a strong warning signal.

❏ Thinks Red Man is a polemical tract by Kate Millett on male chauvinism among the American Indians.

❏ Thinks Jane Fonda should run for president.

❏ Is a pinched-lipped type who hums "I Am Woman" while thumbing through the latest issue of *Ms* magazine.

❏ Reads aloud to you from the minutes of her latest NOW meeting while waiting to pounce on your every chauvinist slip.

❏ Hates football.

❏ Is into martial arts and can quote long passages from *Sexual Politics*

Total score_____

If your potential squeeze scores 2 or more on the above items, that constitutes an Automatic Disqualification and there's no need to proceed further. Tell her your CIA unit has been reactivated and hit the road, Jack.

THE COMPANION SUITABILITY SCALE—Part B

Proceed with this section only if the examinee successfully negotiated Part A. Score 1 point for each item checked and place the total score in the space provided below.

❑ Looks like a *Playboy* centerfold.

❑ Knows the *Kama Sutra* by heart.

❑ Interested in doing research on
  Kama Sutra II

❑ Loves football.

❑ Thinks a pig roast is a cultural highlight.

❑ Makes good money.

❑ Makes good chili.

❑ Thinks it's culturally enriching for you to spend time in your favorite beer joint.

❑ Is delighted when you watch sports on TV for hours.

❑ Loves going to dinner at your favorite barbecue shack.

❑ Regards it as her manifest destiny to keep your refrigerator stocked with beer.

❑ Thinks the tobacco stains on your shirt are quaint.

Total Score_____

Interpret the score on Part B as follows:

Score	Instructions
10-12	This is a real find. All systems go.
8-9	A likely winner. May require some development and re-training.
6-7	A marginal performance. May have possibilities but will require careful cultivation and educational development.
3-5	Red flags go up. A real challenge for conversion, with prognosis guarded at best. Don't unpack.
0-2	Head for greener pastures.

Note:

If subject scores 6 on Part A and 0 on Part B, notify FBI and local security forces before fleeing.

These guidelines should prevent your making a serious miscalculation of the kind so tragically re-counted in Chapter 18. Of course, as you increasingly adopt your Good Ol' Boy persona, your attractiveness to females will mushroom. Therefore you must be prepared to cope with hordes of adoring women. But then life always requires some sacrifices.

CHAPTER TEN

YOUR SMILE LIGHTS UP MY DAY

or
Mastering the
Possum-Eating Grin (P.E.G.)

No issue has occupied the leading minds of this country any more than the attempt to understand the Possum-Eating Grin (PEG). Certainly the difficulty encountered in defining it thus far has done much to weaken the move to establish a national Possum-Eating-Grin Day—this despite a significant groundswell of support for such a holiday in Congress where the grin is widespread, especially during election years.

While its uses in the political arena are widely recognized, the PEG is also a vital part of the Good Ol' Boy's interpersonal arsenal. It's a badge that identifies you to other Gobbies. Wimmin find it especially intriguing, which makes it useful in birddogging.

Getting back to definitions, leading theoretician Roy Blount, Jr., described the grin in Crackers as based on shame and listed Jimmy Carter's smile as an example of it.[1] Now Roy, Jr., is undoubtedly a Good Ol' Boy of fine repute, but as NFL linebackers

---

[1]Roy uses the term "Shit-Eating Grin," a more formal appellation frequently employed in academic and literary circles. Since one aim of this book is to avoid highly technical terms, the more prosaic label "Possum-Eating Grin" has been chosen.

are wont to say to referees, "I must demur." First off, Jimmy's smile wasn't really a Possum-Eating Grin, though it may have had elements of it. His was more a nervous reaction, like a tic. Be that as it may, the heart of the grin is paradox, a quality noted before in the Gobbie makeup.

The paradox of the grin lies in the fact that it expresses contradictory messages at the same time. Your face is being pulled in different directions by opposing forces. This smile says that maybe you've done or are thinking something slightly wicked and are feeling apologetic and at the same time amused about it. It is a half-guilty and yet half-mischievous expression, a simultaneous statement of sheepishness and pride. The PEG is self-effacing and yet defiant. If there is a hint of shame, it is highly leavened with secret delight. In a word, the grin is raffish, linked directly to the Gobbie's eternal quality of boyishness.

This smile is the Good Ol' Boy's silent message to the world, saying let's not take things, ourselves included, so seriously that we forget to have a good time. In short, if you can't work, at least raise a little hell.

Popularization of the PEG should serve to end the unfortunate discrimination to which possums have long been subjected. The rap has been that they are not overly blessed with smarts: "A possum ain't got enough sense to get out of a storm of horseshit." Outrageous jokes have abounded: "Why did the chicken cross the road? To show possums that it can be done." Scurrilous epithets have proliferated: "Dumb as a possum." Recent research by Professor

J. B. "Greenbeans" Detweiler has shown possums to be highly intelligent, moving this eminent scholar to dub them the "porpoises of the trees."[2] Detweiler has further proven that possums' high mortality rate on our highways is due not to stupidity but to their tendency to suffer intermittent bouts of depression during which they become suicidal.

To alleviate this tragedy, it will be necessary to bring possums more into the mainstream of everyday life, thus increasing their self-esteem. This effort is currently being spearheaded by the First Lady's pet project, the laudable TAPL movement (Take a Possum to Lunch). Those interested in participating should call the White House directly. Screening for the program is being handled by the Secret Service so volunteers can look forward to being contacted promptly.

Thus the Possum-Eating Grin has become not only a merit badge of Good Ol' Boy achievement but also a mark of heightened social awareness. Those displaying the PEG will not only enhance their Gobbie image but will also perform a commendable service to society.

[2]Professor Detweiler is currently engaged in exciting new research which explores the possum's ability to comprehend language and communicate with human beings.

THE POSSUM-EATING GRIN

The handy illustration above will be helpful in learning the basics. Mastery may require considerable effort, but remember that the Possum-Eating Grin is the window to your fun-loving soul. Therefore, at least in the beginning, frequent practice in front of a mirror is recommended.

1. The "Double Cup" technique refers to:
   (a) an article of female clothing.
   (b) drinking beer and chewing tobacco at the same time.
   (c) a method of serving demitasse.
   (d) a new way of panhandling.

2. A brogan is:
   a) a classic opening play in chess.
   (b) a connoisseur of fine cheeses.
   (c) a coarse leather work shoe.
   (d) a required move in women's gymnastics.

3. For casual affairs such as a visit to your bookie's office, you might choose:
   (a) a good pair of track shoes.
   (b) a mask.
   (c) something borrowed and something blue.
   (d) the "Main Street Bobby Lee" ensemble.

4. A nice optional touch with the "Broadway Jimmy Joe" outfit might be:
   (a) a wig disguising your identity.
   (b) a Bella Abzug-style hat.
   (c) a baseball cap.
   (d) leg chains.

5. Contrary to macho myth, Good Ol' Boys like:
   (a) to dance the fandango.
   (b) to cook.
   (c) joining the Don Ho Fan Club.
   (d) wearing tutus when at home.

6. The section on "Standard Recipes" was provided to help you:
   (a) drive your wife out of the house.
   (b) repel insects.
   (c) develop a new synthetic fuel.
   (d) prepare for fancy soirées.

7. In choosing a mate, you'll want to find a woman:
   (a) who's heavily into chanting and brown rice.
   (b) who can be one of the boys and yet remain feminine.
   (c) who makes a trumpeting sound when hungry.
   (d) who was past president of the local chapter of the Indira Ghandi Fan Club.

8. Before entering into a significant relationship with a female:
   (a) check her teeth.
   (b) make sure she likes to polka.
   (c) check her blouse for food stains.
   (d) evaluate her on the Companion Suitability Scale.

9. The heart of the Possum-Eating Grin is:
   (a) paradox.
   (b) mental deficiency.
   (c) moral turpitude.
   (d) the decline of the West.

10. The PEG can be helpful in
    (a) getting you committed.
    (b) leading to a divorce.
    (c) identifying you to other Good Ol' Boys.
    (d) providing grounds for your deportation.

Score 10 points for each question answered correctly.
See Appendix for correct answers.

CHAPTER ELEVEN

WHEELS

or
What to Drive

On the road to authentic Good Ol' Boy status, it is vital that you choose an appropriate set of wheels. In cars, as with women, you want to stress sound engineering and high performance. Your choice should be utilitarian and unostentatious, unless, of course, you are engaging in a little high camp; in that case, haul back and let fly with anything that comes to mind.

For projecting your down-to-earth masculine qualities, the basic vehicle and big-time point-getter is the pickup truck. A gun rack can reinforce your "great hunter" image, and a hutch in the back for your bird dogs complements this nicely. You don't actually have to own any dogs. Also, try to have a bag of Red Man or your favorite chaw on the dash and an old copy of *Field & Stream* on the floorboard. A bumper sticker touting your favorite football team is desirable as well.

If you are a little down on your luck financially, an old, deliberately grungy pickup conveys a sense of independence and fulfills your requirements for style and transport admirably. Be seen getting out of it in a tuxedo, and you are flirting with the stuff of legend.

Four-wheelers and utility vehicles generally rank high on the preferred list, conveying a nice sense of

CLASSY CHASSIS

rugged utilitarianism. Sports cars and various kinds of convertibles also project, to an extent, the required cavalier image.

Avoid ostentation. If you drive a Mercedes or other "haute" machine, try and keep it fairly dusty, as though you use it for bird hunting. Also, a bumper sticker saying "Eat More Possum" [1] is a nice touch that will keep even the classiest automotive feet planted firmly on the ground.

The following list of approved vehicles is based on recommendations provided by a panel of experts headed up by J. B. "Greenbeans" Detweiler. Each of these automobiles has been awarded the Good Ol' Boy Tall Hog at the Trough Award for automotive excellence.

[1] A bumper sticker saying "TAKE A POSSUM TO LUNCH" is also acceptable.

Mucho Macho Machines

Lamborghini Countach

A true thoroughbred, this classy beast will quickly serve notice that you've arrived and that your Good Ol' Boy credentials are firmly intact. With 455 horsepower and 7000 rpm, this baby tops out at about 180 mph. It's a steal at only $130,000; pick one up on the way home.

Ferrari Testarossi

This is a stormhog that looks to be doing about 60 mph when parked. So hot it has two radiators, the Testarossi sports a 13.3 sec. quarter-mile time at 107 mph. The top speed of about 180 ain't no slouch either, so keep a little "whip-out" in reserve to pay your speeding tickets.

Porsche 959-"Comfort"

A world class thundershoat, this baby sports a twin turbo-charged, double-overhead-camshaft, 6-cylinder opposed engine which pumps out 450 hp at 6500 rpm. This boar can do a quarter mile in 12.2 sec. and lolls along on the top end at about 195 mph. At only $250,000 apiece, you can pick up a pair in matching colors, one for you and one for your squeeze. ("Yeah, Mr. Trump? You don't know me, but I was calling you about floating a little loan.")

Lotus Turbo Esprit

For handling as nimble as a quarter horse, this steed ranks right up there with the best. A joy to drive, the Esprit blends comfort and performance in a mix designed to stoke the fires in any Good Ol' Boy's

83

automotive heart. Sporting a 4-cylinder turbocharged engine which produces 215 hp at 6250 rpm, the Esprit does a quarter mile in 15.3 sec. With a top speed of 150 mph, this is one classy chassis that's designed to get you to the pig roast on time.

BMW M1

For style and comfort as well as some root hog performance, the trusty M1 will be hard to beat. These classic lines house a nifty 6-cylinder engine with twin overhead camshafts and 24-valve overhead development. It will do a standing quarter mile in 14.5 sec. at about 100 mph and tops out at around 155 mph.

Ferrari F40

To really hit the highway to heaven, pick up on one of these 478-hp road rockets from our friends at Ferrari. Egged on by two water-cooled turbochargers, this Italian stallion will pop the quarter mile in about 12 sec. flat and will do low-level strafing runs at around 200 mph. Pop the clutch on this baby and you could end up in orbit. On top of all that performance, the F40 is about the best looking thing you'll see running around on four wheels; a great combination for a Good Ol' Boy dream machine. Order now to avoid the rush.

At a somewhat more prosaic level, the following vehicles meet the Gobbie criteria for transport quite nicely.

Chevy 4WD Sportside

Named "Four Wheeler of the Year" by *Four Wheeler* magazine, this stout little steed has a standard 4.3-liter, fuel-injected Vortec V6 engine and 5 on the floor.

Ford Ranger STX High Rider
Sports a fuel-injected 2.9-liter V6 engine and optional 4-wheel drive. This classy looking little workhorse will shift into 4-wheel drive on-the-go at any speed with its nifty 5-speed manual transmission.

GMC Sierra 4x4
Has a 6.2-liter, fuel-injected engine, Stanadyne fuel filtration and fuel conditioners along with a Delco Advanced Suspension System. Sporting around in this beefy full-sized pickup, all you'll need to complete the package is an "Eat-More-Possum" bumper sticker.

Suzuki Samurai
A sporty but rugged little 4x4 warrior that's just the ticket for conveying the special Geisha girl in your life to a pig roast or your favorite oasis (or both).

Jeep
From the Comanche to the Renegade to the trusty CJ-5, these time-honored steeds have Good Ol' Boy written all over them.

Nissan Hardbody SE 4x4 truck
This sharp looking stallion offers a 3-liter, fuel-injected engine which provides a hearty 5000-pound towing capacity. With the double-steel wall cargo bed and 2000 pounds of hauling capacity, you'll be

a tall hog at the trough when it comes to carting kegs of beer to the next pig roast.

As in any important life area, there are certain things you'll want to carefully avoid. A slip-up here can get you branded as the automotive equivalent of a Boy George fan:

❏ a cute little stuffed animal in your rear window

❏ a sign saying "Baby on Board"

❏ booming stereo speaker in window

❏ "cute" objects (i.e., furry dice) hanging from your rearview mirror

❏ glitter-style paint jobs

❏ blaringly loud mufflers on a street vehicle

❏ gaudy hood ornaments

❏ a foxtail hanging from your radio antenna

With the above guidelines, you're now ready to polish up your image as a member of the automotive elite. The right set of wheels can move you into the fast lane to Good Ol' Boy authenticity, a sure-fire way to shift your lifestyle into overdrive. Gentlemen, start your engines.

CHAPTER TWELVE

"GIVE ME THAT OLD TIME ROCK & ROLL "

—BOB SEGER

or
The Right Music

THE BEAT GOES ON

J.B. "Greenbeans" Detweiler has said that the way to a man's heart is through the gonadotrophic hormone. Others of a philosophical bent maintain that the best route is through his stomach, while yet another group claims that the supreme pathway is via music.

Whatever your view, the importance of selecting appropriate music in cultivating your Good Ol' Boy identity is undeniable. For example, if you listen to much chamber music with lots of flutes and oboes, you might ought to keep it a secret; whipping your pickup into the faculty parking lot at MIT with Herb Alpert playing on the tape deck would rank with being caught chewing Hubba Bubble or being seen at a Boy George concert. Now a little Hank Williams, Sr., emanating from that deck would be a different story entirely.

To find his kind of music, the Good Ol' Boy turns increasingly to the past. The old songs resonate with memories of simpler times and the nostalgia of old friends and loyalties. In addition, turning back to the oldies represents the Gobbie's distaste for such modern musical touches as filthy lyrics and the glorification of violence.

Specifically, Good Ol' Boys revere the rock and the Rhythm and Blues of the fifties and sixties, traditional blues, and country and western.   In particular, the blues is, like the Good Ol Boy', embedded in life, coming straight at you, with no fluff. When B. B. King sings "The Thrill Is Gone," you can damn well believe that that sucker has left town.

Along with the blues, the outlaw music of Willie Nelson, Jerry Jeff Walker, and Waylon Jennings strikes deep chords in the Good Ol' Boy soul and warrants an important role in your acculturation process. Dwight Yoakum and George Strait are also recommended. Going back a bit further, check out Marty Robbins, especially the gunfighter ballads, and, of course, the ultimate avatar of down-home shitkickery, Hank Williams, Sr.

Preferred groups include Alabama, The Oakridge Boys, Lynrd Skynrd, Creedence Clearwater Revival, the Allman Brothers, Steely Dan, Little River Band, and the Eagles, to name only a few.

It is also crucial to your development that you gain the heightened social awareness so common to Good Ol' Boys. To that end, several ditties that make important social statements are presented. This is in answer to the scurrilous, pinko charge that Gobbies are concerned only with fishing, swilling beer, and watching ballgames and *not* with the important issues of the day.

So on a more somber note, the "Good Ol' Boy's Guide to Songs of Social Protest" is offered. There follows a representative galaxy of stars in the "Good Ol' Boy Musical Hall of Fame," and, finally, the distinguished registry of classics known and revered in musical circles as "The Horseshit and Gunsmoke Hit Parade" is presented.

SONGS OF SOCIAL PROTEST

"She Took the Goldmine and I Got the Shaft"
   —Jerry Reed
(The Good Ol' Boy anthem. An important statement on the new spirit of cooperation between the sexes. Backup vocals by Kate Millett, Betty Friedan, and Norman Mailer.)

"Work with Me, Annie"
   —The Midnighters, 1954
(Important statement in support of women's rights in the workplace.)

91

"Annie Had a Baby"
   —The Midnighters, 1954
(An ode to the joys of motherhood in a context of feminist liberation.)

"Henry's Got Flat Feet"
   —The Midnighters, 1955
(Moving saga of handicapped individual's struggle for recognition as a tap dancer; subsequent TV pilot starring John Travolta never got off the ground.)

"Your Cash Ain't Nothin' But Trash"
   —The Clovers, 1954
(Adopted by the National Association of Stockbrokers as their official song following the market crash of October, 1987.)

"Tutti Frutti"
   —Little Richard, circa 1956
(Beginning with the transcendant lyrics, "A whop bop a loo mop a bop bam boom," this song eloquently endorsed the importance of learning a foreign language. It was subsequently criticized by some on the Right as promoting one-worldism and other views of the Trilateral Commission.)

"Fat Meat Is Good Meat"
   —Memphis Minnie, circa 1930
(A stirring indictment of discrimination against overweight individuals. Subsequently adopted by Weight Watchers as their official anthem.)

"The Chicks I Pick Are Slender, Tender, and Tall"
   —Louis Jourdan, 1942
(A moving lament about the saga of the chicken

farmer in America. Later given the Silver Spur Award by the American Poultry Association.)

"Whiskey, Women, and Loaded Dice"
—Sticks McGhee, 1953
(A poignant ballad chronicling the struggles and sacrifices of American politicians. Later adopted by Congress as official theme song.)

"You Oughta See Grandma Rock"
—Skeets McDonald, 1956
"Rock, Granny, Roll" —The Midnighters, 1956
"Grandpa Stole My Baby" —Roy Brown, 1953
(This trilogy made an eloquent statement about the status of the elderly in America. "Grandpa Stole My Baby" became the fight song of the Gray Panthers. A popular music video based on a medley of the three numbers, starring Congressman Claude Pepper and featuring great dance routines is now available.)

"Mothers, Don't Let Your Babies Grow Up to Be Cowboys" —Waylon Jennings and Willie Nelson, circa 1980
(A stirring exposé of oedipal strivings within the cowboy movement. Soon followed by the poignant sequel, "Mothers, Don't Let Your Sons Grow Up to Be Cowgirls.")

"Rock, H-Bomb, Rock"
—H-Bomb Ferguson, 1951
(A trenchant indictment of the arms race. It's rumored that a punk rock version by Bertrand Russell exists in underground circles, but to date the author has been unable to substantiate this.)

THE GOOD OL' BOY MUSICAL HALL OF FAME

Remember that any list like this is always incomplete and should be viewed as a representative sample to which you may add as you choose.

Founding Fathers	Blues Kings *(and Queen)*
Fats Domino	B. B. King
Chuck Berry	Howling Wolf
Elvis Presley	Muddy Waters
Jerry Lee Lewis	Aretha Franklin
Big Joe Turner	
Bo Diddley	
Ray Charles	
Amos Milburn	

Rock/Rhythm and Blues

Billy Ward and the Dominoes	The Coasters
Lightning Hopkins	The Clovers
John Lee Hooker	Otis Redding
Big Bill Broonzy	The Midnighters
Mose Allison	Gatemouth Brown
T-Bone Walker	The Dominoes
Wanda Jackson	The Drifters
The Charms	

Country and Western

Hank Williams, Sr.	Waylon Jennings
Merle Haggard	Marty Robbins
Webb Pierce	Tom T. Hall
Willie Nelson	Loretta Lynn
Jerry Jeff Walker	Hank Williams, Jr.
Jimmy Buffet	Alabama
Oakridge Boys	Kenny Rogers
Dolly Parton	Emmy Lou Harris

Others

Buddy Holly	The Band
Allman Brothers	Marshall Tucker Band
Eric Clapton	Charlie Daniels Band
.38 Special	Billy Joe Royal
Creedence Clearwater Revival	

THE HORSESHIT AND GUNSMOKE HIT PARADE

These selections are listed in no particular order. Again, many fine classics will have been left off.

"Fever" —Little Willie John
(The best, if not the most popular, version of this classic.)

"Good Rockin' Tonight" —Elvis Presley
(Actually, any of the Sun records could have been on this list.)

"One Scotch, One Bourbon, One Beer" —Amos Milburn
(A great unsung artist, whose classic numbers— "Walkin' Blues," "Roll Mr. Jelly," "Bad, Bad Whiskey," and "Let Me Go Home, Whiskey"—are jewels in any Gobbie collection.)

"One Mint Julep" —The Clovers
(One of several R&B classics by this group.)

"Fujiyama Mama" —Wanda Jackson
(A true rock and roll classic by a truly great, if unheralded, rocker.)

"Our Romance Hit a Sour Note When She Got Me By the Thote" —J. B. "Greenbeans" Detweiler

"Whole Lot of Shakin' Goin' On" —Jerry Lee Lewis

"Chain of Fools" —Aretha Franklin

"Maybelline" —Chuck Berry

"*Smokestack Lightning*" —Howling Wolf

"*The Thrill Is Gone*" —B. B. King

"*She Took the Goldmine and I Got the Shaft*"
     —Jerry Reed

"*I'm Your Hoochie Koochie Man*" —Muddy Waters

"*Your Cheatin' Heart*" —Hank Williams, Sr.

"*Money Honey*" —The Drifters

"*The Year Clayton Delaney Died*" —Tom T. Hall

"*There Stands the Glass*" —Webb Pierce

"*Whiskey, Women, and Loaded Dice*" —Stick McGhee

"*Rock Me, Baby*" —Johnny Otis

"*Hearts of Stone*" —The Charms

"*Sixty Minute Man*" —The Dominoes

"*Drinkin' Wine, Spo-Dee-o-Dee*" —Wynonie Harris

"*Lonely Weekends*" —Charley Rich

"*Hound Dog*" —Willie Mae Thornton

"*I'm Walkin*" —Fats Domino

"*The House of Blue Lights*" —Ella Mae Morse

"Margaritaville" —Jimmy Buffet

"El Paso" —Marty Robbins

"Chantilly Lace" —The Big Bopper

"Let's Have a Party" —Wanda Jackson

So there you have it, sports fans, a Good Ol' Boy Guide to musical fulfillment. For those of you with a scholarly bent, there are several references that might prove interesting. Particularly recommended are those by Nick Tosches, who many feel is the best writer dealing with the music scene today.

Hellfire (The Story of Jerry Lee Lewis), Nick Tosches
Country, Nick Tosches
Unsung Heroes of Rock 'n' Roll, Nick Tosches
The Rolling Stone Illustrated History of Rock and Roll
Honkers and Shouters, Arnold Shaw
The Rockin' Fifties, Arnold Shaw

Many of the old classics are hard to find. One company that's a good source of what's available and will even send you a free newsletter is Downhome Music. They specialize in reissues, so drop them a card. Uncovering these old gems is worth the effort.

Downhome Music, Inc.
103 San Pablo Avenue
El Cerrito, California 94530

And that, folks, is the name of that tune.

CHAPTER THIRTEEN

DO YOU HAVE THE NEW FIELD & STREAM?

or
What to Read

The reading matter that you are seen to have lying on the floorboard of your pickup can be an important factor in strengthening your Good Ol' Boy credentials. So if you've got a copy of *War and Peace* down there, be sure and have a bag of Red Man lying near it so people won't think you're getting biggety or cosmopolitan.

Not that you want to be anti-intellectual exactly, but you should prefer things with a straightforward plot and plenty of pictures. Obviously, magazines are the item of choice. They are also nice in that you can get them all crumpled and stained with chili and tobacco juice and not have to worry about turning them in to some hatchet-faced librarian.

Librarians are probably okay, but they mix with Good Ol' Boys like oil and water. They always seem so prim, proper, and mildly disapproving—the kind of folks who eat a lot of natural foods, go to foreign films, and drink hot tea all the time. You always feel guilty dealing with these people, especially when you're turning in books late or asking a question. Let's face it, there you are, the terminally-arrested adolescent with this possum-eating grin on your face, staring at this ascetic with horn rims who probably just finished *Ulysses* for the second time and who's giving you this condescending little smile that says "You actually had to ask that!?" Probably not a lot of Good Ol' Boys end up being librarians.

Not that libraries don't have their advantages. They have magazine sections and there's usually a number of good-looking wimmin walking around, especially if it's on a university campus. Drawbacks are that you usually can't eat, drink beer, or spit tobacco juice on the floor. There's much to be said, though, for kicking back in the library with your sockless penny loafers propped up on a chair, thumbing through the latest issue of *Soldier of Fortune*, and watching the passing parade.

AT THE LIBRARY

Now that libraries have been covered, here's a brief guide to writers, books, and magazines that will set you on course in the literary area. While the emphasis is on a rugged, down-to-earth style, Playboy and Jackie Collins' novels have been included in order to maintain your intellectual credentials. Of course, any such guide can only provide a smattering of the available material. Once you have a feel for the appropiate literature, you can expand the lists on your own.

> ### THE GOOD OL' BOY'S GUIDE
> ### TO LITERARY EXCELLENCE

Magazines

It is important to keep abreast of important periodicals of the day. The following selection should put you in the vanguard of the literary elite.

Freshwater Fisherman
Field & Stream
Outdoor Life
Bass and Freshwater Fishing
Salt Water Sportsman
Fishing & Boating
Outside
Boating
Popular Mechanics
Music City News
Country Music
Muscle & Fitness
Iron Man
Street & Smith College Football Annual
Street & Smith Pro Football Annual
Street & Smith College Basketball Annual
Street & Smith Pro Basketball Annual

The Sporting News
Sports Illustrated
Inside Sports
Sport
Road & Track
4-Wheel & Off-Road
Motor Sports
Stock Car Racing
Farmer's Almanac
Playboy
Country Song
  Roundup

Authors

For the more ambitious readers among you, the following writers in some way tap into the Good Ol' Boy spirit.

Roy Blount, Jr. - Has a strong Good Ol' Boy flavor in *Crackers* and *What Men Don't Tell Women.* Don't miss the wonderfully informative chapter on "Possumism" in the former.

Dan Jenkins - Author of *Semi-Tough* and *Life Its Ownself.* Creator of Billy Clyde Puckett and the boys. Need anything more be said?

Larry L. King - Warm, humorous, and down to earth in the best Good Ol' Boy tradition. His *None But a Blockhead* is wonderful.

Lewis Grizzard - Very much in tune with what the Gobbie movement is all about. Don't miss his *Elvis Is Dead and I Don't Feel So Good Myself*

Ludlow Porch - An Atlanta Good Ol' Boy who combines warm country humor with a reverence for traditional values and the past.

John Steinbeck - Strong, compassionate, unpretentious. A great Gobbie-style writer, equally adept with a pen, a drink, or a fly rod in his hand.

Pat Conroy - exudes the warmth and rhythms of a Good Ol' Boy.

Mickey Spillane - A classic Good Ol' Boy whose tough-guy books aren't afraid to distinguish between the good and the bad guys; has now achieved acclaim as an actor in Miller Lite commercials.

Nick Tosches - Outstanding chronicler of the music scene with emphasis on lots of material favored by Gobbies. Perhaps his best book is *Hellfire*, the story of Jerry Lee Lewis.

Joe Bob Briggs - *A Guide to Western Civilization, or My Story* and *Joe Bob Goes to the Drive In.*

Jackie Collins - For the intellectual.

Of course, the bedrock of your literary interests will continue to be the sports page of your local newspaper. From that fount of wisdom, all else flows. Remaining current on the sporting stats will solidfy your position among the ranks of the truly informed.

104

CHAPTER FOURTEEN

THE JOYS
OF CULTURE SHOCK

or
Get Me to the Pig Roast
On Time

PIGMALION

Nothing is more inspiring about the Good Ol' Boy movement than its devotion to high culture, to those epochal works in the arts and letters that speak to man's noblest instincts and dreams. It follows, then, that in your quest for Gobbie actualization, the development of a keen cultural awareness is *de rigueur.*

You can enhance your development by studying the works of those luminaries who have already shone in the cultural firmament. The list that follows is therefore offered not only to honor outstanding achievement, but also to provide a beacon that will light your path to refinement. Be guided by these examples and before you can say P. T. Barnum, you'll be tippy-toeing through the tulips of civility in a veritable ecstasy of aestheticism.

The Good Ol' Boy

POET LAUREATE
Rodney Dangerfield

BOOKS

Elvis Is Dead and I Don't Feel So Good Myself —Lewis Grizzard

Crackers —Roy Blount, Jr.

Life Its Ownself —Dan Jenkins

COMEDIANS
Tip O'Neill

SONGS
"She Took the Goldmine and I Got The Shaft" —Jerry Reed

TELEVISION
"The Honeymooners," "Amos N' Andy," Series "NFL Football," "NCAA Football," "Austin City Limits," "Magnum, P.I." (reruns), "Spenser for Hire" (reruns), "Night Court," "Cheers," "Black Sheep Squadron" (reruns), "Bonanza" (reruns), "Sporting Life," "Bassmasters," "Monday Night Football," "The Rockford Files" (reruns)

ACTORS
John Wayne, Clint Eastwood, Bubba Smith, Rodney Dangerfield, Robert Mitchum, Foghorn Leghorn, Slim Pickens, Charles Bronson, Sylvester Stallone, Chuck Norris, Burt Reynolds, Bobby Duvall, Paul Newman, Robert Urich, Tom Selleck,and James Garner.

MOVIES
"Shane," "Hondo," "High Noon," "Hud," "Sands of Iwo Jima," "Back to Bataan," "Sex Games of the Very Rich," "Red River," "Abbott & Costello Go to Mars," "Delta Force," "Rambo," "Attack of the Killer Tomatoes"

PAINTERS
Willie Grice, Grice's Paint & Hardware, Claymore, Idaho (doesn't do shutters)

SYMPHONY ORCHESTRAS
Root Boy Slim and the Sex Change Band

COMPOSERS
Weird Al Yankowitz

HIGHWIRE ARTISTS
Gary Hart

TV COMMERCIALS
Miller Lite, Bartles & James

Cultural Hall of Fame

WATER BALLET
Wilbur Mills, Fanny Foxxe

COMIC STRIPS
"Our Boarding House with Major Hoople," *The Congressional Record*, "Pogo"

PHILOSOPHERS
Casey Stengel, Hugh Hefner, Dr. Ruth, Yogi Berra

BEER JOINTS
The fact that two of the establishments listed here lie in the author's hometown is purely coincidental. Both of these fine retreats have topped Drunken Heintz's recommended list for the past three years.

Sloan St. Taproom, Clemson, S.C.
It has good cold beer and a top ranking by *Lifestyles of the Poor and Ignominious*. As an imaginative added attraction, the cockroaches have been trained in acrobatics. Watching these clever creatures caper and cartwheel on your table is an experience not to be missed. Owner-Janitor Jimmy Howard is now preparing a program in which the talented bugs high dive into mugs of beer.

Polo Lounge, Beverly Hills Hotel
The draft beer's a bit on the warm side, but the Slim Jims and pickled pig's feet are still the best in town.

Esso Club, Clemson, S.C.
Described by the *The Atlanta Constitution* as the best bar in the South.

Tavern On The Green, New York City
The popcorn is always fresh and they change the sawdust and peanut shells on the floor at least once a month.

GREAT QUOTES
"We have the best politicans money can buy." —Will Rogers

"Take it off, take it all off." —Gypsy Rose Lee

"Don't let your mouth write no check your tail can't cash."
—Bo Diddley

"If you ask for trouble, it usually ends up accepting the invitation." —J.B. "Greenbeans" Detweiler

PHILANTHROPIC ORGANIZATIONS
Society For the Nullification of Uppity Behavior (SNUB)
The Leona Helmsley Society

109

There you have it, folks, a galaxy of stars to light your way to the cultural heavens. To further accelerate your progress, a list of top-drawer social activities is now provided. Add these to your agenda and your patina of Good Ol' Boy polish will glow like a possum's eyes shining in your headlights just before the moment of impact.

MAJOR CULTURAL EVENTS	
Pig Roasts	Country and western concerts
John Wayne film festivals	
	Bluegrass Festivals
Three Stooges film festivals	
	Frog jumping contests
Annual Spittoono Festival, Clemson, SC	
	Tractor pulls
Miller Lite commercials	Chili cookoffs
Bass Tournaments	Horseshoe pitches
Chuck Norris movies	Tailgate parties
Foghorn Leghorn cartoons	Fish Frys
MISCELLANY	

Good Ol' Boy Chic

To a Gobbie, a chic is something that grows up to be a chicken which he then fries and eats.

The Good Ol' Boy and Art

Art Who?

Now that your creative juices are aboil, let's move onto the important terrain of "chawing down," a section that will help you really get your teeth into the whole matter of Gobbie acculturation.

CHAPTER FIFTEEN

PARDON ME, SISTER, WHERE'S THE SPITTOON?

or
The Red Man Reaction

Of the many joys of being a Good Ol' Boy, chewing tobacco has got to be near the top. First off, it's great for your image. That telltale bulge in your jaw will confer a mark of manly distinction immediately recognizable to one and all. Second, it can be great for creating that sense of paradox and mystery referred to earlier. For example, the bag of Red Man on the dash of your Mercedes or in the pocket of your tuxedo can add just the right touch. Finally, on a philosophical-spiritual level, there's nothing like the solid feel of a plug in your jaw to let you know that all's right with the universe.

The steps involved in chewing are very simple. First, use loose tobacco, specifically that which is cut into strands. This is by far the cut of choice and is sold in colorful bags like Red Man which has an attractive picture of an Indian on the front. There are several good brands, but Red Man appears to be the favorite.

Second, you reach into the bag and grab a bunch about half the size of a golf ball and place it back in the corner of your jaw. Check in the mirror to make sure the bulge is noticeable. If not, you may have to add some. That side of your face should resemble a chipmunk with the mumps.

Third, you don't really chew the tobacco, but let it sit there dispensing its nectar. Which brings us to step four, which is remembering to spit occasionally. Swallowing the juice can be a laudable macho gesture but can lead to certain gastric unpleasantries.

After you've mastered the basics, it's time to move up to the advanced stage by learning the "Double-Cup Technique." This strategy is a great social facilitator in that it enables you to enjoy a plug in virtually any social situation, from a bull session in your favorite beer joint to a black-tie soirée at the White House.

DOUBLE CUPPIN'

As the name implies, you use two large plastic cups, preferably bearing the logo of your favorite brew or football team. One cup holds your beer, and you spit tobacco juice in the other. It's useful to spit out excess tobacco juice before taking a gulp of beer in order to keep the juice-to-beer ratio to a minimum. Also, as you start to mellow out a bit, be careful you don't confuse the cups and swill a hearty blast of tobacco juice. That can be rather bracing.

There are some important rules of etiquette in chawing down. Namely, don't spit on the floor, in anyone's beer, or out the window of your truck. Such a breach of decorum could get you branded as a redneck, a fate akin to being thought a punk rocker. If you are with a date, always offer her a chaw before you plug in. Also, if she's in formal attire, it's definitely gallant to offer her a bib.

If you find that you can't stand the taste of tobacco, but want to keep up appearances and maintain your Gobbie credentials, you can employ the "'Hubba Bubble Shuffle." Put simply, you fake it with bubble gum. Some companies have even obligingly produced gum already cut into tobacco-like strands. You'll have to be very cautious when spitting or inserting a plug lest you risk detection and subsequent ridicule. One solution is to fill a Red Man bag with Hubba Bubble. Of course, that can prove a trifle embarrassing if someone asks you for a chaw.

CHAPTER SIXTEEN

THIS SPORTING LIFE

or
What Time's the Kickoff,
Little Mama?

A LITTLE SNACK BEFORE THE GAME

An avid appreciation of sports is a crucial element in your Good Ol' Boy identity. Thus, you'll want to be up on the latest games, scores, standings, etc., prior to going into your favorite watering hole. Once there, never ask who's playing on TV but hurry out muttering something like, "Damn if I didn't leave my

Red Man in the truck." Get hold of a paper and quickly check the TV listings.

The following are a sampling of sports-related cultural events that delight Gobbies everywhere and will certainly enhance your image as a social mover and shaker.

Tailgate Parties

These are usually held in parking areas before football games and can be major social happenings. Fried chicken and potato salad are staples, and you can even bring your own charcoal grill for cooking steaks or hamburgers. Set up your bar in the back of your pickup and you're in business. Invite guests and display your knowledge of game-related trivia. It's desirable to have at least two stickers on your car boosting the local team.

The Pre-Game Rally

The pre-game champagne or Bloody Mary brunch is a great setting for Good Ol' Boy conviviality and can add greatly to your credentials. It is preferably thrown within walking distance of the stadium. Make this a lawn party so you can hail other Gobbies on their way to the game and you have the makings of a social coup.

The Post-Game Rally

You try to exit gracefully without someone stepping on your hand.

The Football and Chili TV Party

This is a great event for days when there are multiple games on TV, thus making for an all-day affair. You'll need to have at least two TV sets hooked up. Key ingredients are cold beer, chips, dip, and Redeye Chili (see recipe in food section). Plan to start cooking bright and early in the morning—that'll be half the fun. This format is also useful for adding a social touch to other televised cultural events like professional wrestling or the Daytona 500.

Since catching the games on TV is such an important cog in your Good Ol' Boy cultural wheel, it is important that you master appropriate spectating techniques. The following styles will greatly enhance your hours in front of the tube and solidify your image as an armchair jock nonpareil.

Styles for TV Watching

1. Easy Rider: Sitting upright with both hands free to shovel in beer, chips, hot sausages, etc. Cowboy boots up on coffee table.

2. Kicked Back: Completely prostrate in recliner. Your squeeze or live-in French maid stands by to place beer and chips in your mouth. Disadvantage: Unwanted complaints from the "peanut gallery" (i.e., wife, girlfriend, mother-in-law, their biggety friends, etc.).

3. The High Tech: No female necessary, since you have a robot installed beside the recliner. The motion of opening your jaw activates a sensor which

121

signals the robot to sequentially insert Fritos and several ounces of beer.

Midnight at the Oasis

Although football is emphasized here, other spectator sports like basketball, baseball, and the Solid Gold dancers loom large on the Good Ol' Boy agenda and are prime targets for viewing at your favorite watering hole. Again, it's vital to keep up on your statistics so as to always appear knowledgeable. ("Hell, Hawg hit .381 last year. Don't know what's wrong with the boy this season.")

Suiting Up

Actually playing sports can be very gratifying. Golf (pronounced "goff") and team efforts like softball are among the favorites. Contrary to popular belief, many Good Ol' Boys are avid tennis players, but activities that involve a number of people are somewhat more advantageous in that they can be tied in with subsequent roistering at your favorite oasis. Playing on the local rugby team is useful in that it's good for your macho image, and you can put really interesting bumper stickers on your pickup like "Playing Rugby Takes Leather Balls."

Contrary to myth, Good Ol' Boys are into a wide variety of cardiovascular exercises such as running, aerobics, and *watching* the Jane Fonda fitness video. In addition, Gobbies have traditionally gained distinction in a number of Olympic events such as the barhop, broad jump, breast stroke, and the 12-ounce curl.

With this chapter under your belt, you are well on the way to becoming a sports legend in your own time. Now that you are in the swing of things athletically, sprint on to the next chapter and find out how to break away from the pack in the large organization.

CHAPTER SEVENTEEN

ROOM AT THE TOP

or
Success and Survival
in the Big Organization

$\mathbf{P}$erhaps no other environment can be as stifling to the freewheeling Good Ol' Boy spirit as the arid wasteland of the large business or governmental organization. Bureaucracies tend to be particularly odious hives of human pettiness and folly, and in order to thrive in them you are going to have to play by a different set of rules. In short, a special game plan is required whether it regards the way you speak, dress, or any other aspect of your personal style.

If you are caught up in one of these monoliths, unless you are the boss or have the good fortune to be in an organization run by other Gobbies, you will have to take precautionary measures to preserve your Good Ol' Boy lifestyle and your sanity. This is especially true if you happen to be in one of those reactionary environments where you are actually expected to devote a significant part of the day to work.

Fortunately, a clever plan can thwart even the most stupefying bureaucracy. Thoroughly familiarizing yourself with the following remedial strategies should enable you to maneuver your way up the organization with the agility of a greased pig. First, a look at basic organizational structure.

If you are in an outfit dominated by other Good Ol' Boys, you're in hog heaven. The actual flow chart of a major corporation is reproduced below in order to give you an idea of what this kind of setup looks like schematically. To assist you in analyzing the power structure in your own work environment, you may want to create this kind of chart. Remember that the company shown below represents a near ideal which may be difficult to duplicate in every situation.

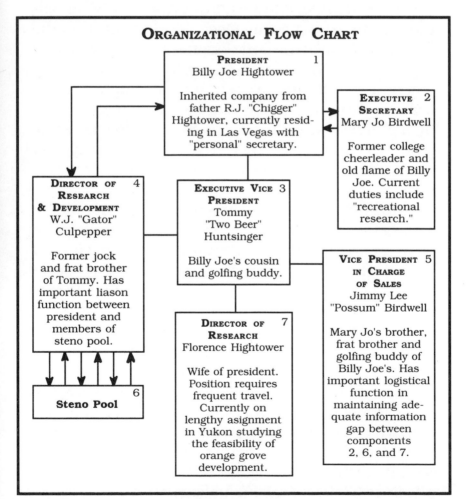

ORGANIZATIONAL FLOW CHART

PRESIDENT 1
Billy Joe Hightower

Inherited company from father R.J. "Chigger" Hightower, currently residing in Las Vegas with "personal" secretary.

EXECUTIVE SECRETARY 2
Mary Jo Birdwell

Former college cheerleader and old flame of Billy Joe. Current duties include "recreational research."

DIRECTOR OF RESEARCH & DEVELOPMENT 4
W.J. "Gator" Culpepper

Former jock and frat brother of Tommy. Has important liason function between president and members of steno pool.

EXECUTIVE VICE PRESIDENT 3
Tommy "Two Beer" Huntsinger

Billy Joe's cousin and golfing buddy.

VICE PRESIDENT IN CHARGE OF SALES 5
Jimmy Lee "Possum" Birdwell

Mary Jo's brother, frat brother and golfing buddy of Billy Joe's. Has important logistical function in maintaining adequate information gap between components 2, 6, and 7.

Steno Pool 6

DIRECTOR OF RESEARCH 7
Florence Hightower

Wife of president. Position requires frequent travel. Currently on lengthy asignment in Yukon studying the feasibility of orange grove development.

Moving Up

Unless you are already in the upper echelons, your main goal as an organizational Good Ol' Boy must be to reach that ultimate bastion of security, your own private office with a secretary out front guarding the approaches like a Doberman Pinscher. This is a defense perimeter comparable to that of the Chicago Bears, behind which you can relax, secure from prying eyes and unwanted phone calls. In this inner sanctum you can maintain a sane schedule, perusing the sports page in peace and even cranking up a plug of Red Man if you feel the urge.

THE INNER SANCTUM

Reaching this haven will require great adroitness and a careful plan of action. The Strategic Maneuvers Program was developed at the Harvard Business School and should provide you with just the blueprint you need for your climb to the top of the pecking order. It begins with the important issue of time management and goes on to cover such vital areas as looking busy, shuckin' and jivin', office etiquette, and handling problem situations.

Time Management

To the Gobbie on the move in the pressure-cooker world of big business or government, nothing is more crucial than the effective utilization of time. Blocking out time for important matters requires the self-discipline to schedule and prioritize. As an example of excellence in time allocation, here is an actual schedule provided by a high-level executive in a major governmental bureaucracy:

Activity	Time Allocated (in minutes)
Drinking coffee	36 min.
Reading sports page	30 min.
Filling out parlay card	24 min.
Reading financial section	30 min.
Chatting on the phone with stockbroker	15 min.
Attending unnecessary staff meeting	45 min.
Organizing office football pool	39 min.
Work	30 min.
Lunch	90 min.
Flirting with secretary	18 min.
Planning Saturday's golf game	24 min.
Filling out excessive and unnecessary government forms	54 min.

130

Fixing up boss with the new fox in steno pool	24 min.
Calling bookie	18 min.
Calling loan officer at bank	21 min.
Calling finance company	24 min.
Work	39 min.
Calling the girl in Records you met at the office party	24 min.
Meet with boss to pass on football tickets and data on steno-pool fox	24 min.
Total	10.15 hrs.

Note that in the preceding example, you have worked over-time, evidence of exemplary devotion to duty. This marks you as a "comer" and will not be unnoticed by upper management.

Looking Busy

In large organizations appearance is all. Therefore, the importance of looking busy cannot be over-emphasized, especially when you actually have little or nothing to do. The following techniques were developed specifically for use by Good Ol' Boys in these situations and should greatly enhance your image as a veritable human dynamo.

1. Form committees, attend meaningless meetings, and write lengthy obfuscatory memos on obscure topics. Confer endlessly with co-workers over petty details and regulations.

2. Photocopy articles from trade journals and circulate them to co-workers. Don't worry that you haven't read the material. No one else will either.

3. Read the latest Jackie Collins novel encased in a trade journal. Nod sagaciously and doodle on a scratch pad as if taking notes.

4. Call the weather number and carry on a forceful business conversation for the benefit of all within earshot.

5. Walk briskly from one area to another carrying a clipboard and a batch of computer printout sheets.

Shuckin' and Jivin'

As you begin your ascent up the organizational ladder, there are a number of image-enhancement techniques which can greatly speed your progress. Master these moves and you'll be tap dancing your way to the top with the ease and agility of a Gene Kelly.

The Cupid Ploy:

Fix up your boss with the new fox from the steno pool. This can greatly enhance your image as a deal maker as you negotiate between the two regarding time, place, etc., and establish you as an indispensable link in the organizational chain.

The Thinker Maneuver:

Carry a copy of *The Wall Street Journal* into the office with you each day and keep it prominently displayed on your desk. Keep a copy of *In Search of Excellence* in evidence and occasionally browse through it during lunch. This will identify you as a heavy thinker and make it easy for you to dazzle colleagues and top management with streams of meaningless doubletalk.

The Quick Pitch:

Through whatever means necessary, obtain football tickets to crucial games for the big cheese in the organizational hierarchy. This will promote your image as resourceful and well connected. In addition, the top dog will come to associate your face with the pleasure and ego inflation of receiving good tickets to key games.

The Magic of Graphs:

Dream up an endless array of graphs which purport to show things like increased efficiency, productivity, cost control, staff possum consumption, etc., etc. Present these at meetings with an appropriate spiel of jargon and gobbledygook. Organizational types are mesmerized by graphs and though no one will have the foggiest notion of what yours mean, they will be baffled and amazed by them, greatly adding to your aura as an office guru. Preface the punch line in your presentation with a phrase like, "And as anyone can readily see..." and you're home free.

Pulling the Rip Cord:

Agility is as important in the workplace as it is in athletics. The ability to nimbly bail out of a nosediving

133

PULLING THE RIPCORD

project or department in your organization is crucial to your success. Make your move early, claiming the press of overwork, the desire for new challenges, or the laudable impulse to give an unsuspecting co-worker the "opportunity." When the crash comes, you'll be safely ensconced on the high ground, shuckin' and jivin' your way to the executive suite.

Office Etiquette

An important rung in your ladder to the top is a thorough awareness of organizational etiquette. In an atmosphere where appearance is all, appropriate personal style is essential. No two areas are more important than how you dress and speak.

Dress for Success:

This is one area in which you'll need to sink a significant portion of your spendable cash or even go in the hole. You'll want to come on as a clothes horse, understated but top drawer. Stress expensive three-piece suits in conservative colors or pinstripes, with an occasional tweedy blazer thrown in. These glad rags must convey an air of impending success which will draw others to you like a magnet.

Knowing what not to wear is also important in managing your organizational wardrobe. Avoid wearing bib overalls to work unless your CEO does. Also to be avoided is a popular style known in fashion circles as the "Lounge Lizard" (see Chapter 7).

Learning the Lingo:

Nothing can put a Good Ol' Boy on the inside track in the mega-organizational sweepstakes faster than mastering an appropriate manner of communi-

THE GREAT ENLIGHTENMENT

cation. Again, it's a triumph of style over content in that how you talk will be far more relevant than what, if anything, you are saying. In fact, the preferred strategy in large organizations (and politics) is to speak most impressively while actually saying nothing. To that end, there are a number of effective techniques you can employ.

A. The Strategic Phrase: An important weapon in your verbal arsenal is the high-sounding phrase which actually cloaks a more prosaic message. Now you know and they know what you mean, but part of the game is that no one ever acknowledges this. In addition, you are protected from ever being pinned down as actually having said anything. Some examples with translations are provided below.

Strategic Phrase	Translation
"It is vital to the successful implementation of policy that we achieve a unity of vision and purpose."	"You turkeys need to get the story straight before the auditors arrive."
"An awareness of our mandate from the taxpayers (shareholders, etc.) is crucial to appropriate resource allocation."	"We've got to realize that we can only get away with so much crap here."
"We need to achieve a consensus on the optimal interdepartmental interface."	"Look, yahoo, stay off of our turf or I'll send those pictures from the office party to your wife."
"It's important to become aware of informational lacunae within the organizational personnel structure."	"You peckerwoods don't know your asses from third base."
"Don't misunderstand me, I think it's a great idea. I just have a problem with certain minor aspects of it."	"That load of crap is going to fly about as well as a cement mixer."
"I can say without reservation that the current management has my unqualified support. With the implementation of our new operating plan, I am fully confident that we are well on the way to achieving our goals."	"This crew of jive asses couldn't chew chewing gum and walk at the same time. You can be sure that I'll be hitting the silk long before this bush-league operation totally goes in the tank."

B. The Art of Double-Talk: When you want to revert to total verbal camouflage, the ability to spout meaningless, circular gobbledygook is invaluable. Not only will this technique enthrall your co-workers and superiors, it will prove very helpful in dealing with the media as you move up the ladder. The following example was excerpted from a committee report given by a Good Ol' Boy in middle management in a large corporation. He was soon promoted and was eventually recruited for a top position in a major governmental bureaucracy.

> " It is crucial in fulfilling our obligation to the share-holders that we carefully assess, while concurrently, of course, maintaining an awareness of and sensitivity to personnel factors which importantly impact productivity, which we must realize flows from the dynamics of the strategic interface of diverse input and skills, this considered horizontally, and of course the vertical, hopefully bi-directional input of the various organizational levels. I have here a simple graph..."

C. Now You See It, Now You Don't: In constructing your rhetorical house of mirrors, you'll want to make liberal use of jargon. Buzzwords like "the public interest," "transcendent mission," and "organizational dynamics," while essentially meaningless, will quickly establish you as a heavyweight thinker and put you on the fast track to the executive suite.

Overcoming Problem Situations

Occasionally, when faced with an overzealous boss, you may be forced to resort to a strategy known in organizational circles as "The Surprise Party." This ploy does require a certain logistical flair in that you will have to coordinate the proper setting, the

138

services of two female consultants, and a photographer. It is recommended that the strategic photographs obtained be filed in a special location away from the workplace.

SURPRISE PARTY

With this chapter under your belt, you should be ready to ascend the organizational ladder of success faster than a hedgehog with a hot foot. After a little quiz to test your perspicacity, we move on to the gripping saga of a Good Ol' Boy who fell from Grace. (And you shoulda seen Grace!)

POP QUIZ 6

1. A grungy old pickup can:
   a) get you stopped by the police.
   b) let people know you're down and out.
   c) help you qualify for food stamps.
   d) convey a sense of independence and style.

2. A nice touch on the floorboard of your truck might be:
   a) a dead lizard.
   b) an old copy of *Field & Stream.*
   c) a picture of Bella Abzug.
   d) a poison-pen letter from your ex-wife.

3. In music, Good Ol' Boys are:
   a) listening to a lot of old records by Hermione Gingold.
   b) going punk.
   c) clamoring for a revival of the Sex Pistols.
   d) turning increasingly to the past.

4. The "gunfighter ballads" were recorded by:
   a) Liberace.
   b) Kate Smith.
   c) Marty Robbins.
   d) Tina Turner.

5. A major advantage of libraries is that you can:
   a) enrich yourself intellectually and culturally.
   b) kick back with a magazine and watch the wimmin.
   c) often have a stimulating chat with a librarian.
   d) check out wonderful recordings of operas and chamber music.

6. A plug of tobacco in your jaw will:
   a) increase your dental insurance.
   b) make it hard for you to get dates.
   c) cause hair to grow in your palms.
   d) confer an air of manly distinction.

7. The "Hubba Bubble Shuffle" refers to:
   a) substituting bubble gum for tobacco.
   b) the latest production of the New York City Ballet Company.
   c) a heretofore undiscovered Wagnerian opera.
   d) Congress explaining a tax increase to the American public.

8. "Midnight at the Oasis" refers to:
   a) a meeting of the OPEC ministers.
   b) the beginning of the camel-breeding season.
   c) an excuse often employed by Arab husbands.
   d) watching sports on TV at your favorite watering hole.

9. The "Strategic Maneuvers Program" is:
   a) a popular book on succeeding with the opposite sex.
   b) a blueprint for moving up the ladder in a large bureaucracy.
   c) a sex education manual.
   d) an investment guide written by Bunker Hunt and Jim Bakker.

10. "Shuckin' and Jivin'" refers to:
   a) what your stock broker does when you try to pin him down.
   b) a classic move in water ballet.
   c) a number of image-enhancement techniques.
   d) the content of *The Congressional Record.*

Score 10 points for each question answered correctly.
See Appendix for correct answers.

CHAPTER EIGHTEEN

A SHOCKING
TRUE CONFESSION

or
How I Became An Effete Snob

"I HAVE SINNED"

She seemed so nice at first. I actually met her at a football game. She filled out those jeans so perfectly that I didn't notice that her date looked like a refugee from Haight-Ashbury circa the sixties. It should have registered when she read a Gore Vidal novel during most of the game, and I must have repressed the snatches of chamber music that I heard from her Sony Walkman. Oh God, I should have known!

We had our first date the next evening, and she seemed to enjoy the pig roast. She even had some beer and chili, but I do remember now her hair being in a tight bun and seeing an occasional condescending smirk on her face. But she filled out that cotton blouse so vibrantly that I must have been blinded. Later that night at her place the trap was sprung. She *did* know the *Kama Sutra* by heart.

She scored a six on the Companion Suitability Scale, but I thought she would shape up and at first there seemed to be progress. She actually went to a country and western concert with me and watched a couple of ballgames on TV—but it was all a cruel hoax.

Things deteriorated quickly. At first she talked me into going to the ballet because she "already had the tickets." Once there, it was insidiously easy to go along with everyone else and pretend I enjoyed it. Then there was the meeting of something called the "Alternative Lifestyles Solidarity Committee," and after that it seemed as though there was a committee for every day of the week.

The horror deepened. I actually attended a flute recital with her on a night I was to meet the boys down at the local oasis. I knew I was in big trouble when we went to a foreign film one Saturday afternoon instead of using my football tickets. But, oh, those nights! The brainwashing process had taken hold. I was addled and bemused, my will as soggy as a hotdog bun in a steamer.

Things went steadily downhill from there. There were chamber music concerts, poetry recitals, and macrobiotic food; I even found myself leafing through a copy of *Ms* magazine. Then there were the wine and cheese parties with her friends. Suddenly I found myself bemoaning the lack of "culture" and making snide remarks about people who were "unsophisticated" enough to enjoy sports. Blaming everything in the world on the United States started to seem intellectual and superior. It was thrilling as we all dropped phrases memorized from *The New Yorker* and *The New York Times Book Review*.

Oh, the shame of it. I gave up Redman because she said it was gauche. I hadn't eaten any chili or barbecue for weeks. I was staying at her place nearly all the time and was even pretending that her modern art really looked like something native to earth.

I hit bottom on the morning I was to trade in my pickup on a Volvo. Suddenly the awful truth of my degradation hit me full force. Muttering that I was going to the cheese and wine shop, I rushed to my house and called the Good Ol' Boy Tactical Recovery Team. As I sobbed out my story, I could already feel a rush of relief. She must have sensed something because a half hour later she appeared, screaming and waving a copy of *The Female Eunuch*, just as the boys were hustling me into the van.

The reprogramming procedure began immediately with a plug of Red Man. I was rushed to my favorite beer joint where cold brew and Redeye chili were administered while I watched two football games on TV. These were followed by a taped Chuck Norris movie and a couple of hours of country and western music. By the next day I was back to normal and promptly renewed my membership in the Society for the Nullification of Uppity Behavior (SNUB). I knew I was one of the lucky ones. I had survived an attack of effete snobbery.

Chapter Nineteen

Of Minnows and Men and Sunny Sundays

or
One Philosophical Tangent—
Hold the Onions

So there you have it. We've talked about a number of things that make up the soul of the Good Ol' Boy. About love of tradition and respect for a simpler, more straightforward past. About humor, good food, comradeship, and not taking oneself too seriously. About pig roasts and patriotism. And still we're left with a feeling, an approach, a state of mind.

On a recent morning, I drove to a little neighborhood store near my home to get a Sunday paper. The sun was shining brilliantly and I had a mug of hot coffee with me. At the store a man standing outside, wearing a John Deere cap, greeted me warmly and told me about how their minnow tank had frozen the night before. As we stood silently pondering this dilemma, it suddenly seemed as vital to me as anything in the universe. Later, as I was leaving the store, we spoke again and, riding back, I became aware of how crucial it is in an age of pompous glitz and hype to preserve a world where you can go on a sunny morning and get a friendly greeting from a stranger in coveralls and a John Deere cap and talk about a minnow tank freezing and realize that it's important. Riding on, I had the thought that liking and wanting to keep that kind of world has a lot to do with what Good Ol' Boys are all about.

Correct Answers to Pop Quizzes

Pop Quiz 1:
1. c	2. d	3. e	4. c	5. d
6. d	7. b	8. d	9. b	10. b

Pop Quiz 2:
1. c	2. c	3. d	4. d	5. d
6. c	7. d	8. d	9. a	10. c

Pop Quiz 3:
1. d	2. d	3. b	4. b	5. b
6. d	7. d	8. a	9. d	10. c

Pop Quiz 4:
1. d	2. b	3. c	4. a	5. c
6. b	7. d	8. c	9. a	10. b

Pop Quiz 5:
1. b	2. c	3. d	4. c	5. b
6. d	7. d	8. d	9. a	10. c

Pop Quiz 6:
1. d	2. b	3. d	4. c	5. b
6. d	7. a	8. d	9. b	10. c

Photo by Bill Ellis

David Cannon was born in North Carolina and is now a clinical psychologist in private practice in Clemson, South Carolina. Prior to settling down among the South Carolina good ol' boys, Dr. Cannon studied at the Royal Academy of Dramatic Art in London and was for a time a Hollywood scriptwriter, actor and producer.